TAKE CHARGE OF YOUR CREDIT

STRATEGIES TO BOOST SCORES, REDUCE DEBT, AND CREATE FINANCIAL FREEDOM

RILEY WHITMAN

Copyright © 2025 BY SYNAST PUBLISHING

Published by SYNAST PUBLISHING

All rights reserved.

ISBN: 978-1-968418-47-2

Table of Contents

TAKE CHARGE OF YOUR CREDIT

INTRODUCTION

In a world where financial health is increasingly tied to credit scores, understanding and managing credit becomes not just a necessity but a strategic advantage. Many individuals find themselves overwhelmed by the complexities of credit management, often feeling trapped by past financial mistakes that continue to haunt their credit reports. The emotional weight of poor credit can impact not only purchasing power but also the broader scope of one's financial freedom and peace of mind.

This book is designed to be a comprehensive guide for anyone looking to take control of their credit profile, offering both a roadmap to improve scores and a toolkit for reducing debt. It starts by breaking down the fundamentals of how credit works, demystifying the opaque systems used by lenders and bureaus. By understanding these systems, readers can transition from feeling at the mercy of their credit scores to actively shaping their financial destinies.

The narrative is not just about theoretical knowledge but focuses on actionable strategies. Readers will find step-by-step instructions on accessing and interpreting credit reports, disputing errors with confidence, and leveraging legal rights for protection. Practical advice is paired with interactive tools to keep track of progress, such as budgeting apps and credit score monitoring services.

Moreover, this book tackles common fears and misconceptions head-on, addressing issues like the myth of "quick fixes" and the dangers of falling for predatory scams. It emphasizes the importance of patience and persistence, guiding readers to celebrate small victories on their path to financial recovery. By setting realistic expectations and providing a clear action plan, the book empowers readers to transform setbacks into comebacks, reinforcing the idea that financial freedom is a journey worth undertaking.

Ultimately, "Take Charge of Your Credit" serves as both a mentor and a motivator, encouraging readers to become proactive stewards of their financial futures. With dedication and informed action, anyone can move beyond the shadows of debt and credit issues to achieve a stable, secure financial life.

R I L E Y   W H I T M A N

TAKE CHARGE OF YOUR CREDIT

1

UNDERSTANDING CREDIT AND ITS IMPACT

The Basics of Credit

When it comes to personal finance, credit is one of the most important concepts to know. Credit is a key element in any person's financial arsenal, and it has its opportunities and challenges. Simply put, credit is how reliable a person is in taking money and paying it off as expected. Credit scores and reports measure this trust and are important in determining an individual's financial opportunities.

The logical basis of credit is very simple: you get money now in order to pay it back later, usually with interest. The principle takes numerous shapes, like credit cards, loans, and mortgages. All these products enable people to cover urgent financial demands and spread the price across time. However, that ease of credit comes with the cost of paying on time, which directly influences creditworthiness.

The credit ecosystem is made up of a few key actors: lenders, credit bureaus, and data furnishers. The money is lent by lenders such as banks and credit card companies, and the terms of its repayment are determined. Data on credit behavior is collected by credit bureaus like Experian, Equifax, and TransUnion and is used to create credit reports. The information provided to these bureaus about the history of consumer payment is furnished by data furnishers who may be utility companies and landlords.

Lenders and credit bureaus rate consumers on a number of data points. One of the most important aspects is payment history, credit use, and credit history term. The history of payment, the promptness, and the regularity of payment are crucial as they are the embodiment of reliability. The ratio between credit used and credit available is credit utilization, and this is used to show how people handle their financial obligations. Credit history length gives information on long-term financial behavior, and the longer the history is, the more likely it is to be stable.

It is also important to learn how credit scoring models work. The most common scoring systems across the lenders are the FICO score, which is an industry standard, and the Vantage Score, which is a newer model. Both models have their own calculation technique and consider similar factors: payment history and credit utilization. Understanding which score a lender operates with can help consumers focus their attention on the most topical data points.

Credit scores have more than just borrowing implications. These impact the capability to have a home, a job, and even utility services. A high credit score may translate to preferential credit terms and low interest payments, and a low score may translate to increased costs and opportunity costs. Therefore, financial health is not the only sphere of influence of credit.

People have to be active in order to navigate the credit environment. It includes checking credit reports on a regular basis and ensuring their accuracy, comprehending what factors impact scores, and making wise financial choices. In this way, consumers can operate within the credit system instead of being dependent on it and eventually gain more financial autonomy and security.

How Credit Affects Your Life

Credit is a basic part of modernity, which is interwoven into our existence in the financial sphere. Its impact is not only measured in the number of figures on a piece of paper, but also affects different aspects of our lives and determines our opportunities and options. At the heart of it, a credit score is an expression of trustworthiness in numbers, a manifestation of perceived trustworthiness in the eyes of lenders, landlords, and even prospective employers.

The implication of credit scores stretches a long way. Using a good credit score as an example, in taking a loan to purchase a house, good interest rates can be guaranteed, and the monthly payments are affordable. On the other hand, a low score can lead to an increase in rates, thus adding to the financial burden. This has spilled over to car loans, where interest and loan approval opportunities are equally impacted.

In addition to loans, credit scores are important when renting apartments. This can be seen in the fact that landlords tend to rely on credit scores to determine the trustworthiness of potential tenants. One may have a good history of paying on time and displaying responsible credit use, which may be beneficial in a rental application. Still, a low score can lead to a higher security deposit or even a complete denial.

Credit scores can also affect employment opportunities. In some instances, particularly in the financial industry, credit reports are used as a measure of reliability and financial responsibility in an applicant (Michaels, 2009). Having a poor credit history could be a signal as to whether a person is able to handle their duties or sensitive data.

Even utilities are affected by credit. This can be based on credit record, or deposits can be requested, or service can be denied. This applies to phone services and even insurance premiums, whereby credit scores would influence the rates being quoted.

The price of bad credit is real and important. An increase in interest rates charged on loans can add thousands of dollars to expenses incurred over the years.

The bigger picture of having a good credit score is the missed opportunities, including failing to get an apartment or a job of choice.

The road to credit insight and redemption is not easy, however. There are many myths, including the one that carrying a balance on a credit card will help to improve scores, or that a person will hurt their credit if they look at their own credit report. These myths have the potential to misguide people and stifle their economic development.

Good credit is a process of patience and making good decisions. It takes a lot of effort to establish and sustain a good credit score; this can be achieved by paying on time, maintaining low credit card balances, and only trying to secure credit when you need it. With time, such habits lead to a good credit history, leading to access to more advantageous financial opportunities and protection.

The credit story is an empowerment story. Given the impact of credit on different facets of life, individuals can take initiatives to better their financial status. Such empowerment is achieved through knowledge and strategic deployment of credit tools and resources, as well as a feeling of control over one's financial destiny. Simply put, credit is not a numerical figure; it is a critical component that can be used to influence the path that one may take in life greatly.

Common Misconceptions

There are numerous myths floating about credit scores and credit management that can unknowingly impair financial gains in many individuals. The common myth is that a balance on a credit card is required in order to build credit. Not only is this idea false, but it can also give rise to unnecessary interest payments and debts. Actually, it is better to pay off the balance every month in order to keep the credit score healthy, as it shows that the credit is used responsibly and no interest is applied.

The next myth is that looking at their own credit report will make their credit score lower. This is the fallacy of confusing the difference between soft and hard inquiries. Soft enquiries, including those where one checks their credit themselves, do not have any impact on the credit score. Having said that, hard inquiries, or those that are made when a lender performs a credit check for a loan or credit application, can have a small influence.

Another misconception that many individuals have is that income affects credit scoring. Although income is a factor that lenders use to determine repayment capacity, it does not find a place in the calculation of credit scores. The factors used in determining credit scores include payment history, credit utilization, length of credit history, and so on, but not income.

It is also believed that clearing debts will automatically raise his or her credit score. Although debt repayment is definitely a good thing, it does not immediately remove the negative entries on a credit report. Depending on the nature of the debt and the general credit profile, this may have different effects on the credit score. An example of this is that paying off a collection account cannot take the account off the report. Still, it can prevent additional damage and demonstrate to future lenders that the account holder is dedicated to paying off debts.

Moreover, other people believe that after seven years, all debts are taken off credit reports. Most negative information, such as late payments, defaults, etc., is usually deleted after seven years; however, exceptions do exist. The example is that bankruptcies might stay on a credit report for as long as ten years. These are the most important timelines to understand in order to address expectations and establish credit repair plans.

The second myth to consider is the understanding that a credit score will be significantly reduced when an individual applies to take out new credit. New applications may cause a temporary decline, but that is normally insignificant and fleeting. Even in cases where new credit is responsibly used, the score will go higher with time as the total available credit increases and the utilization ratio improves.

They are individuals who need to be educated to realize these illusions in order to improve their economic status. These myths can only be busted through education and awareness. People need to look for credible facts from credible sources and consider consulting financial advisors or credit counsellors to understand the credit scoring procedure better. This way, they are able to make informed decisions that are in tandem with their financial objectives and also eliminate strategies that might appear productive but end up being counterproductive. They are pitfalls that can be avoided and will lead to an improved financial base and credit history in the long run.

Setting Realistic Expectations

Finding a middle ground in the world of credit repair, it is essential to know the realistic possibilities and limitations. In many cases, people embark on this trip, full of hope, because they have been promised fast solutions and immediate products. However, realistic expectations are the key to sustainable development and the avoidance of disappointment pitfalls.

The appeal to instant credit enhancement is easy. Offers and advertisements that claim to raise credit scores drastically in a short period of time are especially tempting. However, such assertions tend to ignore the realities of credit repair. It is imperative to note that developing a good credit profile is a slow task, similar to developing a garden where time and continuity of care produce the best outcome in the long run.

The idea of the quick fix is one of the most widespread myths in credit repair. Businesses can ensure that credit scores increase significantly within one month or provide some insider tricks to shortcut regular processes. But such promises are usually deceptive, and in most instances, they are scams. The real credit improvement process requires learning to read credit reports, finding mistakes, and acting in a methodical way to correct them. It is time-consuming and laborious, and a person can get disappointed when they have no success on the first night and may even suffer financial losses.

It is important to know what is possible. Some examples are challenging true negative reports or deleting true late payments, neither of which is likely to be successful. The credit system is to represent a true and fair description of financial behavior. Therefore, it is possible to correct the mistakes and correct information, even when it is negative, which is often left. This is where the emphasis should be on creating good credit habits and not trying to erase mistakes in the past by using questionable methods.

An actual credit repair schedule is often a few months to several years, depending on the situation. It is a process involving various steps like regularly checking credit reports, disputing mistakes, and paying within the stipulated time. All of these activities lead to credit score improvements. It can be a good idea to set milestones and track progress to remain motivated in this journey.

Furthermore, it is important to know how to detect scams. Offers that require upfront payments or that do not provide transparency in their operations should be handled with care. There is no hidden loophole or promise of money in legitimate credit repair work. Rather, they are concerned with providing people with the means and knowledge to be in charge of their credit.

Tenacity and a good measure of doubt work side by side. It can be helpful and motivating to involve the support communities that are viewed as reputable and consult with reliable people and organizations. Experience and education: It can be valuable to share stories and learn about others who have gone through their credit repair experience and been successful.

In cultures, the way to make credit better is to do so slowly, by degrees. When expectations are realistic, they allow a person to have a clear mind and face this challenge with a strong spirit, as it is possible to make progress, though very slowly. Any tiny progress made is a win in its own right, which leads to a better financial future.

2

BUILDING A SOLID CREDIT FOUNDA-TION

Importance of Credit Reports

Credit reports are an important component of the financial ecosystem as they are both an indicator and a predictor of the fiscal well-being of an individual. They represent an entire history of an individual's credit history, including all credit accounts, all loans, and all bill payments, and thus, they are also a representation of how a person conducts himself/herself and how well he/she manage his/her money. It is not just a book of financial operations; it is quite an important device that influences many other factors of normal life because it can precondition the appearance of the most demanded financial goods and services.

Credit reports are important not just because they allow access to credit. They also play significant roles in the decision-making of lenders, landlords, and even employers. Lenders review credit reports when they are seeking a loan or a credit card to determine how risky it is to lend money. Being able to maintain a good credit report can go a long way in helping an individual to find better loan conditions, like reduced interest rates and increased credit limits. On the other hand, a corrupted credit report can lead to increased rates of interest or credit refusal, which directly affects the ability to access money, as well as the ability to buy.

In the case of landlords, credit reports are used as indicators of whether a prospective tenant is reliable and capable of meeting the financial requirements of the rental agreement. The distinction between possessing the right residential house and having a credit record will aid in convincing the landlords that the tenant can handle the financial load. In the same way, potential employers can look at credit reports during the employment process, especially when they are hiring someone to handle financial transactions or confidential information. The aspect of responsibility and integrity may positively reflect on an individual through a solid credit report.

Credit reports are also an important part of financial planning and management. They give people a clear picture of their financial position, which allows them to highlight areas that need to be improved, including paying off current debts or settling late bills. Viewing your credit report regularly can assist you in identifying any errors or evidence of identity theft so that corrective measures can be taken at an opportune time. Its active credit management also plays a significant role in maintaining a good credit score, which is one of the determinants of financial stability.

Besides being useful in practical contexts, credit reports also reflect the larger meaning of financial responsibility. They are a physical reminder of what one has done or has not done with money and what effects this has had on his or her life, and makes him or her feel responsible and therefore makes him or her act wisely in his or her financial dealings. This feature of credit reports makes them particularly educational, as they allow people to understand how their financial decisions influence their creditworthiness in general.

The credit reports are even more important due to the legal rights given to consumers. The Fair Credit Reporting Act (FCRA) gives people the right to access their credit reports, which are readable and accurate. This legal framework will enable the consumer to sue for misleading information and avoid losing their financial reputation.

After all, credit reports are not only a financial document, but a tool of personal and economic empowerment. They help people to negotiate the financial environment with ease, providing them with access to opportunities that can improve their quality of life. Therefore, having the knowledge and means to utilize the power of credit reports, the person turns into a master of his/her own finances, thereby rendering life safe and successful.

Decoding Credit Scores

Although credit scores may seem intimidating, they are actually a simple number that reflects your creditworthiness, boiled down into the intricate fabric of your financial history. These scores are not randomly set and are determined by a host of factors that lenders consider to determine your lending risk. It is important to understand these scores since they determine the interest rates paid on loans, whether or not you can obtain a mortgage, and even whether or not a rental application will be approved.

The most well-known models of credit scoring are FICO and Vantage Score. Though both have the same purpose, they are different in their method of calculation. An example would be the FICO scores, which are the industry standard and created by the Fair Isaac Corporation and utilized by a majority of lenders. These scores are between 300 and 850, and the higher the score, the more creditworthy the person is. Vantage Score, however, was created by the three largest credit bureaus: Experian, Equifax, and TransUnion, to offer a different model of scoring. It also applies a range between 300 and 850, but assigns varying weights to some credit behaviors.

Your credit score is made up of many varied components. The most important one is the payment history, which constitutes about 35% of the FICO score. This is a measure of your history of paying bills on time. This component can be devastating due to late payments, defaults, and bankruptcies. The ratio of the current balances of your credit accounts to the credit limits is the credit utilization, which contributes 30% of your score. A healthy score to keep this ratio under 30 is usually recommended.

Another important factor is the length of credit history, which adds 15 percent to your score. This is an average of the age of your credit accounts, and it rewards you when you have older accounts. Your mortgage, credit card, and auto loan make up 10 percent of your score. There are many types of credit that lenders consider to be good, meaning you can run various forms of credit well. Finally, 10% of your score is made up of new credit. This takes into account the number of new accounts you have recently opened and the number of hard inquiries, or inquiries when a lender is checking your credit to take out a loan.

You can make financial choices using the knowledge of the differences between FICO and Vantage Score. As a pointer, FICO might be more worried about payment history than Vantage Score, which might tolerate a late payment as long as you have been doing better over the years. In addition, certain lenders give a higher preference to one of the scores, based on the kind of credit being requested, like a mortgage or auto loan.

The only way you can keep your credit score under control and improve it is to ensure that you check your credit report across the three bureaus periodically. Appealing against mistakes and errors early enough can help avoid the impact of mistakes on your score. Moreover, you can increase your score gradually by adopting good credit practices such as paying bills on time, minimizing debt, and minimizing new credit inquiries. You can now control your future finances by demystifying your credit score and knowing the elements that make it up, so that your credit score can be truly representative of your financial accountability.

Understanding Credit Bureaus

The art of credit can be doing business in the credit world by realizing the complex position credit bureaus take in our everyday lives. These organizations play a leading role in creating our credit image, determining how lenders see us, and ultimately deciding whether we have access to financial products.

The heart of it all is the credit bureaus, which are agencies that store and gather consumer credit information. They also compile data on other sources, including lenders, creditors, and government documents, to generate a detailed credit report. Lenders rely on these reports to determine whether a person is creditworthy. This landscape is dominated by the three biggest credit bureaus in the United States, Experian, Equifax, and TransUnion, which all have huge databases of personal financial information.

The main purpose of credit bureaus is to give credit reports to lenders, who use the reports to determine the risk of lending money or giving credit. These reports contain the history of credit of an individual, such as the history of credit accounts and payment history, as well as information on any public records, such as bankruptcies or liens. The information collected by credit bureaus assists lenders in making relevant decisions regarding the granting of credit, interest rates, and credit limits.

Credit scores (frequently based on credit reports) are a numerical measure of the creditworthiness of an individual. These scores are calculated by algorithms that take into account many factors on the credit report, which include things like payment history, the amount owed, length of credit history, and the type of credit utilized. The most famous credit scoring systems are FICO and Vantage Score. Although every model works with similar data, the models might exercise different weighting criteria on the same issues, leading to different scores.

This is important because it helps the consumer understand the role of credit bureaus in ensuring that their credit is well-managed. With proper and updated credit reports, people can ensure that their lenders are doing the best they can with their financial habits. It is also advisable that credit reports issued by the three bureaus are reviewed regularly so that the consumer can ensure that the information is accurate and resolve any discrepancies or errors that may arise.

Credit report errors may be made due to a number of reasons, including identity theft, clerical errors, or old information. Consumers can challenge the credit bureau when they have noted some inaccuracies. Under the law, the bureau will then have to investigate and amend any errors proven within a given time. Through the process, there is emphasis on care when handling credit, as errors committed but not corrected can impact credit scores and finances.

Credit bureaus also do ID verification and fraud prevention. They also provide other credit monitoring and credit fraud indicators, and these services could assist consumers in identifying and acting on unauthorized practices in a relatively short time. These tools are invaluable in terms of identity theft protection and verification of the credit report.

Essentially, credit bureaus play the role of guardians of financial information, which shapes diverse financial decisions. When consumers are properly informed about what happens to their data and the functions that their data performs, they can take proactive measures to ensure that they manage their credit health. With a smart approach to credit bureaus, people can improve their credit score and reach their long-term financial targets.

The Role of Lenders

Lenders are considered to be central to the financial ecosystem because they are the gatekeepers of credit and financial opportunities. They are organizations like banks, credit unions, and specialty financial organizations that lend and extend credit facilities to consumers and businesses. The latter entities are not only essential due to their capacity to disburse funding but also due to their impact on consumer financial standing and the credit environment.

The greatest role of lenders is to determine the risk of lending money to people or organizations. This includes the comprehensive assessment of creditworthiness that is based on the examination of numerous factors such as credit scores, income levels, financial history, and so on. This judgment is very important because it determines the conditions of the loan, including interest rates and repayment terms, and finally determines whether the borrower will be able to obtain credit.

Credit scores are important to lenders when making decisions. These are numeric values that denote an individual's credit risk, as collated by credit bureaus. The higher the credit score, the lower the risk, and in most cases, better terms will be given on a loan. On the other hand, a low score would also increase interest rates or even make it impossible to borrow money, and that is why keeping your credit in good shape is so crucial.

In addition to the first approval, the lenders are also expected to report consumer credit activity to credit bureaus. This reporting will include information on payment records, credit use, and defaults of the borrowers, which, respectively, will be reflected in the credit scores of the individuals being borrowed to. Regular and punctual payments can boost the credit profile of a borrower, whereas defaults can have a devastating impact.

In addition, lenders are financial educators, but this is indirect. They bring to the fore the issue of debt responsibility management through the terms and conditions of loans. This includes interest rate knowledge, compounding interest impact, and long-term borrowing impact. This kind of knowledge can help consumers make sound financial choices so that they do not fall into the trap of debt.

Lenders are also important to the wider economy. They stimulate the economy through the provision of funds that enable businesses to grow and consumers to buy homes or cars. Increased consumer spending is a major factor in the economy and an aspect that the availability of credit can affect.

Nevertheless, the lender-borrower relations cannot be smooth sailing. Problems of predatory lending and the availability of credit to disadvantaged populations are still highly pressing. Borrowers can be enticed into debt by high-interest rates and by other indirect costs. To fight this, the government agencies have come up with mechanisms and safeguards to check on fair lending practices.

To conclude, lenders play a critical role in the financial system, providing them with the resources to pursue their financial objectives either individually or in business. They not only transact but also regulate consumer behaviour, how well the economy grows, and the overall stability of the financial market. The role and impact of lenders are one of the most important factors to consider when moving into the world of credit and finance.

3

MANAGING YOUR CREDIT HEALTH

Monitoring Your Credit Regularly

Checking credit regularly is like looking after a vital organ- it's very important but can be easily forgotten. The habit entails an alert attitude to the interpretation of the numerous factors that lead to the financial profile. By monitoring credit scores and credit reports closely, people can guarantee their financial reputation is healthy and does not contain any misleading information or fraud.

It starts with an interpretation of the credit report, which is a complete account of credit history. It contains information on credit records, transaction history, and inquiries, among others. By going through this report on a regular basis, it would be possible to determine whether the information contained in the report is true or not. Even minor mistakes can have a serious impact on credit ratings, which may influence the issuance of a loan or the interest rate.

The frequency and mode of checking a credit score and report are one of the most important elements of credit monitoring. Experts suggest following a disciplined plan, which includes checking the credit rating every month with the help of free applications and examining the complete report once a year. Such a routine keeps a person informed and helps detect any irregularities early enough. Several free and low-priced services with functionality allow sending notifications about new requests or major changes in the credit profile.

In addition to regular checkups, an early warning system to detect identity theft or other unlawful activities can be installed as a notification system to detect any alterations observed in the credit report. These alerts might warn of a new credit request or a sudden change in account balances and take appropriate steps to mitigate the potential damage within a limited period of time. Furthermore, having a bit of understanding of the differences between the different scoring models, like FICO and Vantage Score, a person can make more sense of their scores according to their financial goals.

Credit monitoring also comprises having personal objectives and milestones. Whether it is meeting a new credit score or winning a battle over a mistake, the reward of such success can help inspire further effort. A physical marker of credit progress, such as a journal or a chart, can be a concrete measure of progress and can be employed as a motivational tool.

In addition, frequent credit checks enable one to make sound fiscal choices. It helps them to plan their debts strategically, use credit wisely, and prevent typical traps that can be detrimental to credit scores, like closing old accounts or missing payment dates. People using a proactive approach will be able to become more financially literate and practice with credit.

After all, the process of keeping a vigilant eye on credit is an act of vigilance and empowerment. It reaffirms the need to be informed and prepared and to make credit management more of an active process than a reactive one. It can be achieved through the conduction of periodical checks, which can be used to help secure their financial health, align them with their credit report, and establish a healthy financial base. The practice not only helps fulfill short-term financial objectives but also preconditions long-term financial prosperity and success.

Identifying Errors and Fraud

In the complex world of personal finance, it is important to have a clean credit report. Nevertheless, one must be careful and informed to navigate the pitfalls of mistakes and scams that might tarnish one's monetary reputation. The credit report has been one of the most important documents in fiscal well-being. At one point in time, it has become the cause of lies and falsifications, which could affect credit scores and consequently, the financial opportunities on a grandiose scale.

Mistakes made in credit reports are quite frequent and may be caused by minor clerical errors or more serious problems such as identity theft. These inaccuracies may be in the form of false personal details, e.g., misspelled name or address, or more serious financial anomalies, e.g., accounts that are not owned by the individual, false late payments, or false duplicate accounts. Any of these inaccuracies may unfairly bring down the credit score, and it is thus important that people examine their credit report with utmost care on a regular basis.

The most important step in detecting mistakes is to receive a full credit report of each of the three largest credit bureaus, Experian, Equifax, and TransUnion. The differences between these reports are easier to identify by juxtaposing them. Sections that contain account summaries, credit investigations, and public records should be given further focus as they are the most common areas where errors occur. Discrepancies can be identified early enough before causing harm to the credit score in the long term.

Another defining point of credit health is fraud detection. The common type of Identity theft is one in which a third party takes up another person's identity and utilizes their personal information to open new accounts or to make unauthorized purchases. Such red flags might include accounts or requests that a person has never seen, a credit refusal that appeared out of the blue, or an abrupt credit rating adjustment. People are also taught to insert warnings when they open a new account or when they renew their credit report, because they might issue warnings in time about the malpractices.

It is important that once mistakes or fraud are detected, a prompt move is taken. There must be an option to report the mistake to the credit bureau with written proof of the error. This includes the writing of a dispute letter and any other supporting documents that may prove the allegation of a mistake. The credit bureau then must enquire into the claim within a time frame of usually 30 days. In fraud, a fraud alert or credit freeze is one way of avoiding further illegal access to credit. This is not only beneficial in safeguarding against recurrent fraud, but also acts as a warning to any potential creditors that further verification is required before credit is extended.

Credit monitors can be very useful in the detection and prevention of errors and fraud. These services update their credit activity regularly and alert individuals to changes that could signal mistakes or fraud. Nevertheless, you must select reliable services and avoid unnecessary upsells that provide very little value.

However, in the end, it is a continuous process that takes effort and care to maintain credit health. Learning to spot mistakes and fraud and how to respond will help people to protect their financial health and make sure their credit report is accurate and reflects their financial background. This awareness helps not only to prevent any financial loss but also enables individuals to manage their financial futures.

The Dispute Process

Learning to bypass the dispute process is an important step towards gaining control of your credit. It encompasses a collection of systematic measures that help rectify the inaccuracies on your credit report that can have a profound effect on your financial well-being. The first thing you do is to obtain all the needed documents and proof to back up your cause. This includes a photo ID issued by the government, the current address, any account statements, and any canceled cheques or payment confirmations. It is important to arrange these documents carefully and label every piece of information: everything must be legible and effective in order to present your case.

Another key ingredient is determining how to file your dispute. All these approaches, online, mail, and phone, have their own merits and demerits. Online disputes are fast, but they can be limited in the documents you can post. Cases that are complicated or related to legal documents are mostly sought after instead of by mail, as they can be written down in detail. Telephone conflicts are more of an unwarranted advisory, but may be warranted in some cases. In each method, you need to record your progress carefully by keeping confirmation numbers, certified mail receipts, and call logs so that you can compose a detailed audit trail.

A dispute letter is an art form. The letter should have a clear subject line, personal identification information, an exact description of the mistake, and a direct request to correct or delete it. It is important to keep the style professional, concise, and factual. The supporting documents should have a checklist listing the documents included, which will help prevent any omission on the part of the recipient.

It is important to know what happens next once your dispute is filed. Credit bureaus have a moral responsibility to work out and clarify disputes under the Fair Credit Reporting Act (FCRA) within 30 days. They must inform you of the findings within five days after they have carried out the investigation. The available options are to prove the information to be correct, fix the mistake, erase the false information, or request more information. As a result, you can verify the fixed report, and you can elevate the dispute or appeal in case your claim is refused.

One should be persistent with bureau pushback. Bureaus can either use stalling methods or reject any disagreement with words such as frivolous or irrelevant dispute. It may be important to respond with more substantial evidence or increase the scale of the issue by providing more documentation or references to certain FCRA violations. A demand to produce a method of verification can also be an effective device, and it is legally required that the bureau produce information as to how they checked the information in dispute.

In other cases where the conflicts are not resolvable, a higher regulator, such as the Consumer Financial Protection Bureau (CFPB) or state attorneys general, may have to settle the disputes. Complaining can help speed up the process of investigation and resolution. In the process, there should be an organized paper trail and a tracker because these are key planning methods in successful dispute resolution. With a careful and persistent approach to the dispute process, you have the power to rectify inaccuracies and enhance your creditworthiness, which is the foundation of a safer financial future.

Using Credit Monitoring Tools

With the new digital age, the credit monitoring landscape has grown tremendously, providing consumers with numerous tools that allow them to maintain a watchful eye on their credit health. Free and paid, these tools are invaluable companions on any financial journey you take in the complicated world of personal finance. Knowing how to utilize these resources well can greatly help someone become financially literate and manage their credit.

There are numerous credit monitoring services available on the market, and each has its own set of features and advantages. Available services such as Credit Karma, Experian, Credit Sesame, and my FICO address various consumer needs and offer different sets of data to the user. One would need to understand the difference between these services, especially regarding what they track, given that some of them track credit reports, whereas others track credit scores. This difference matters; credit report monitoring is keeping track of what is happening with your credit report (opening new accounts, inquiries, etc.), whereas score monitoring is keeping track of the changes to your credit score over time.

Real-time alerts characterize effective credit monitoring services. These alerts alert people to any major changes on their credit reports, including new inquiries or account status changes. This live feed enables users to take action against any possible issues, like opening unauthorized accounts and spotting identity theft early enough to keep their credit score intact.

But sometimes all the information about it can be too much. In order to overcome information overload, it is recommended that users create smart alerts and personalize their notifications according to their preferences and needs. It is important to create a reasonable review timeline- choosing monthly versus real-time follow-up can be a way to balance alertness and relaxation.

Despite the usefulness of the mentioned tools, a person should consider the unnecessary upsells and fake security they can claim. There are a lot of services that have extra features at a price, which are not always needed. One should also consider the value that these add-ons actually add, or whether they are just a marketing gimmick. When identity theft is a continuing concern, it may be reasonable to use a paid service, which is frequently more thorough in terms of monitoring and recovery support.

To reap the best of credit monitoring tools without being overwhelmed by them, it helps to consider incorporating these tools as part of a larger financial management plan. This involves utilizing logs and templates to trace disagreements and track developments that may help to observe tendencies and celebrate improvements over time. The periodical, systematic assessment of credit reports and scores can enable them to become active participants in controlling their credit.

Credit monitoring tools are, however, priceless in ensuring you have a healthy credit profile, though they should be applied judiciously in combination with other financial management habits. With the effective use of these tools, people will have more confidence and control when it comes to navigating through the complexities of credit management.

4

IMPROVING YOUR CREDIT SCORE

Payment History Importance

The best component of an excellent credit score is the careful upkeep of payment history. This is the critical dimension in credit management, because, as a matter of fact, this is what lenders have in mind when it comes to the financial credibility of a company. A history of paying consistently and on time is not only a mere formality but also an indication of financial discipline and good financial health that eventually affects creditworthiness.

Upon exploring the complexities of credit scoring models, one can clearly see that payment history contributes a significant share to the overall score computation. This is mostly due to the fact that lenders consider the past behavior of the payment as a good indicator of the financial behavior in the future. One defaulted payment can have far-reaching repercussions that can last a lifetime, including a damaged credit rating. In that way, the significance of an impeccable payment history cannot be underestimated.

The effects of payment history are not linear; on the contrary, they differ according to the period and the rate of delinquency. For example, a 30-day-late payment may appear to matter differently than one 60 days overdue or one that is 90 days overdue. The intensity of the penalty that credit scoring models assign depends on the duration of delinquency, which further highlights the importance of resolving payment issues in a timely fashion. A single missed credit payment is a scar on an otherwise beautiful credit report, telling the lenders that one has become irresponsible with his or her finances.

A number of steps can be taken to reduce the risk of late payments. This is where automation comes in, as people can create automatic payments using banking apps. This guarantees that payments are made on time, at all times, and without manual intervention. Also, a reminder can be helpful with alerts built into the electronic calendar or a cellular alarm, emphasizing payment plans at the center of financial activities.

Another very important strategy is to monitor the due dates of payments. One needs to know about the change in the billing cycle or probable delays in the delivery of the mail that might result in missed payments. A detailed bill due date spreadsheet or checklist may help to create a clear picture of what lies ahead so that it can be acted upon in time. In addition, lapses in payment schedules may be avoided by establishing email or SMS alerts when approaching due dates.

When situations arise where a shortage of cash flow occurs, it is important to manage these problems skillfully in order to pay without default. Some temporary relief may be achieved by calling the creditors to ask them to change the due dates or use a small emergency fund. In addition, exploring opportunities, including getting an overdraft line, will allow them to navigate payments when financially strained without the need to ruin their credit history through default.

Lastly, one of the important credit management aspects and a credit statement to the authority it holds in the future of money is payment history. With the focus on making payments on time and taking some proactive actions to make everything consistent, a person can establish and sustain a good credit profile. Not only precautionary measures, but also the plan to increase the credit rating and accumulate the feeling of control and empowerment with finance contribute to more opportunities for financial resources and stability.

Managing Credit Utilization

In the complex world of credit management, the key element is knowing how to use credit. Use of credit is the relationship between your outstanding credit card balances and the total credit limit. This ratio is an important part of your credit score, and in many cases, it can be very influential in showing your financial health. The low utilization ratio is always good, as it indicates to the lenders that you are using your credit in a good manner and not spending much borrowed money carelessly.

It is impossible to overestimate the effect of credit usage on credit scores. Even when you pay your bills on time, the high usage rate may have a negative impact on your credit score. The reason is that it implies possible overextension and increased default risk in the minds of creditors. So, having a utilization rate of less than 30 percent is one of the widely suggested levels to aim at. This is because when your overall credit limit is 10,000 on all cards, you should only have a total of between 3,000 dollars outstanding.

A number of viable strategies could be put into use to control and maximize the use of credit. One way to do it is to pay more than once a month. You can decrease the amount that is reported to credit bureaus by paying your balance before the statement closing date, which will decrease your utilization ratio, and by requesting an increase in the credit limit. Assuming that this is approved, this will effectively reduce your usage ratio without having to change your spending patterns, as long as you do not spend more money with the higher limit.

Another trick to control utilization is to decentralize purchases over a variety of credit cards, instead of using one credit card. This will assist in maintaining a low balance per card and hence a healthy overall usage ratio. It is also prudent to know the balance of the statement and the credit limit, as well as how utilization is computed on all cards, because the utilization on any single card can affect your total score.

Budgeting and tracking tools may be useful assets in ensuring low credit utilization. You can use apps such as Mint or YNAB (You Need a Budget) to track your expenses and notify you that you are close to reaching your credit limit. Bad Banking Apps can also help you avoid unintentional spending and keep your usage at bay by setting up balance alerts within your banking apps.

Nevertheless, you should be wary of pitfalls that may skyrocket your use. By closing old credit cards, you decrease the amount of available credit so that you will have a higher utilization ratio. Maxing out cards in case of emergencies or keeping them above zero can bring about an increase in the utilization rates as well. These cases should be taken into consideration and thought through.

Credit use and management are not only about ensuring that you have a low ratio but also about making decisions that can impact your credit profile positively. With these strategic practices, you may be able to control your use of credit, thus increasing your creditworthiness and improving your financial prospects.

Length of Credit History

Overall, when it comes to credit scoring, credit history matters a lot in determining your overall credit profile. This feature of credit checks explores the chronology of your credit activity, providing your loan providers with an idea of how you have managed your money in the past and how long they can trust you. The longer the credit history, the stronger the indication of the credit profile, and the more detailed picture of your credit management capabilities.

The next element that is evaluated in the length of credit history would be the age of your oldest credit account. This factor is the basis of your credit history; it is where your credit experience begins. An old history is one of the ways your credit score can be good, because it represents a long history of credit management.

Moreover, the average age of all your credit accounts is determined to give you a balanced opinion regarding your credit history. This average age is of special significance since it represents the maturity of your credit profile in general.

One of the most important elements of having a healthy length of credit history is the strategic management of existing accounts. Having old credit accounts that have been closed, particularly with a long history, can have the side effect of shortening your credit history, thus impacting your credit score. To maintain the length of your credit history, keeping such accounts open even though you may not use them is sometimes a good idea.

The frequency of opening new accounts is another factor to be considered. Although it may be easy to apply for new credit lines to various advantages or deals, sometimes taking up a new credit line may lower the average age of your credit accounts. This decrease may have a potential negative impact on your credit score because a younger age on your credit report can give the impression to the lender of a weaker credit history. In this way, you should find a middle ground between the necessity of new credit and the possible effect on the length of your credit history.

Further, your credit history can affect how you receive new credit, based on the duration of your credit history. A long credit history is something that lenders can easily interpret as a stable and reliable borrower. Such perception can result in better loan and credit card terms, including low interest rates and high credit limits. This is why the longer the credit history, the better your future financial prospects are, as it improves your overall creditworthiness.

In conclusion, a credit history length is a crucial element in your credit rating that shows your financial behaviour and long-term financial stability. You can have a positive impact on this aspect of your credit profile by paying attention to the age of your credit accounts, maintaining older accounts, and opening new accounts thoughtfully. Such a strategic decision would not only help you maintain a healthier credit score but also improve your financial standing as perceived by lenders, opening the door to better credit opportunities.

Mix of Credit Types

When it comes to personal finance, comprehending the details of credit is crucial to every individual aiming to establish or preserve an excellent credit report. The mix of credit types is one of the various elements that make a credit score robust, and in most instances, many consumers do not notice this. Although this element may not seem of much importance in the big picture of credit scores, it can make or break a person in the eyes of his/her lenders.

Credit mix means the type of credit that an individual has, between the revolving credit, like credit cards, and installment loans, such as mortgages, auto loans, or student loans. The logic of this element is quite simple: lenders consider a credit mix of various types as an indicator of financial responsiveness. It shows a borrower is capable of reasonably handling various kinds of credit commitments, and thus needs different approaches to payment and budgeting.

The ever-changing and flexible balance, and the changeable terms of payment, characterize the revolving credit that mostly takes the form of a credit card. Consumers must pay a minimum amount of money every month, but they can pay more or less based on their economic status. This form of credit evaluates the capacity of a borrower to service a continuing debt and a low ratio of the utilization of credit, which is the ratio of the credit being used to the current credit limit.

On the contrary, installment loans are loans that are borrowed in a specific amount of money and repaid over time with equal payments. In this kind of credit, one must be disciplined in making regular payments over an extended period to develop a history of being reliable. Examples of these include mortgages and auto loans, and these loans give the lending institution a clue on whether a borrower will honor long-term financial commitments.

It is the interaction of these various kinds of credit that makes the idea of credit mix essential. A healthy combination of revolving and installment types of credit can ultimately benefit a credit score because it demonstrates to the lenders that the borrower is capable of using different financial products. But it is not just having a number of credit accounts, but also accounting for them.

When those who may want to better their portfolio in terms of credit mix, it would be better to begin by evaluating their existing credit portfolio. Gaps can be found, including installment-loans-only or credit-cards-only, and these may help determine future strategic choices regarding new credit applications. As an option, a credit card user who relies on the use of credit cards as the main financial tool can consider borrowing a small loan in their own name so as to diversify their credit portfolio. On the other hand, someone who has multiple installment loans but no credit cards may be interested in opening a credit card account and putting it to good use.

Diversification in the type of credit may be beneficial, but it must be done cautiously. The number of new accounts applied for in a very short time may result in several hard inquiries on a credit report, which may temporarily reduce a credit score. Also, the opening of new credit lines is only possible when it fits the financial objective and can be handled without excessive stress.

The end game is not simply to improve a credit score but to develop a long-term financial lifestyle that promotes long-term goals. Such objectives and the flexibility needed to add the required credibility can be effectively achieved using the balance of these types of credits. People should be allowed to take significant strides towards financial empowerment using their knowledge and optimization of the credit mix to demonstrate to lenders that they are responsible and competent borrowers.

5

STRATEGIC CREDIT BUILDING

Secured Cards and Authorized Users

Secured credit cards are a step to help a person build or reestablish credit. They work much like regular credit cards, but with one important difference: they involve a cash deposit that serves as collateral and usually defines the credit limit of the card. This deposit helps reduce risk to the issuer, and so secure cards are available even to persons who have poor or limited credit histories.

It is not very difficult to get a secured card. Applicants are usually required to deposit between 200 and 500 dollars, which also serves as their credit limit. Such a structure not only secures the issuer but also gives the user a sense of financial responsibility, as he is in effect borrowing against his own money. In the long term, as the payments are always made on time, users can show that they are creditworthy, and they may be offered to use unsecured credit cards, as a deposit will not be needed.

The type of secured card to use is a matter of choice. Potential consumers will resort to the authorities of goods that can offer certain terms and reasonable prices. Others provide benefits that are akin to regular credit cards, including rewards programs or interest-free grace periods on shopping, provided the balance is paid in full at the end of the month.

Besides having a secured card, one of the tricks to credit building is to become an authorized user of a credit card account belonging to another person. This setup enables the legitimate user to take advantage of the account owner's credit history. The good activities can be reflected in the credit report of the person allowed to use it, like when the primary cardholder is paying the bills regularly, and the use of his or her credit card is minimal.

This is not, however, an easy scheme. What can affect the credit score of the authorized user is when the primary account holder does not manage the account properly by defaulting on payments or reaching a credit limit. So, the financial habits of the main cardholder before becoming an authorized user are extremely important to consider.

To reduce the risk of losses and maximize the gains of being an authorized user, it is better to agree with the major account holder to set certain rules and establish clear communication. By tracking the activity of the account via alerts or periodic review, it is possible to maintain control over the account.

Those who want to include an authorized user have to carefully consider the decision, choosing an account that has a record of using credit responsibly. Also, an exit strategy is a wise idea, so that the authorized user can take themselves out of the account in case of financial abuse.

Secured cards and authorized user arrangements are both potential options when it comes to improving a credit score, though they need to be used strategically and closely monitored. Knowing how to work these tools and use them to your advantage, people can create a strong credit base and open up more financial opportunities in the future.

Applying for New Credit

The path to the application of new credit involves a delicate comprehension of the ways that credit applications might affect financial status. When people think of opening new lines of credit, they need to know that this process will impact their credit scores by creating hard inquiries. A hard inquiry is one in which the lender will look at your credit report to determine whether to loan you some money. Compared to soft inquiries, which are made when you request your credit or when a lender has pre-approved you to receive an offer, hard inquiries have the potential to reduce your credit score temporarily. The difference between these kinds of inquiries is vital to know so that you can prevent any unjustified effects on your credit.

Strategic timing is needed in the area of credit applications. They should take caution when applying for new credit, preferably spacing the applications six to twelve months apart to limit the combined impact of several hard inquiries. This gap can serve to maintain the credit rating, and this can be especially useful when you are planning on securing serious financing, such as a mortgage or auto loan, in the near future. In addition, it is recommended that when a person is shopping around to get rates on a bigger loan, say in mortgages or auto loans, it is best to pool these requests within a short time frame, or more precisely, in a range of between 14 and 45 days. This is called rate shopping, and credit scoring systems tend to bundle up several enquiries within this time frame into a single enquiry, thus minimizing the adverse consequences on your credit report.

Proper assessment of your current financial requirements and how the new credit line will benefit you should be done before applying for any new credit. These include posing some tough questions, like will the new credit allow you to improve your credit utilization ratio, which is the amount of credit you are using versus your total available credit. Reduction of the utilization ratio will have a positive impact on your credit score. Also, think about the benefits in the long term, like rewards, cashback, or reduced interest that the new credit could provide.

But there are traps to watch out for. Opening too many new accounts within a short period of time is one of the most common mistakes that will decrease the average age of your credit accounts and lead to a low score. On the same note, store credit cards, though attractive at first, can have a high interest rate and may not be as beneficial in the long term. Another thing to avoid is the temptation to open an account with a sign-up bonus, as it may result in unnecessary debt and a messy credit profile.

A balance between timing, strategic planning, and awareness of one's financial objectives helps one to manage new credit applications effectively. With an informed approach to the process, people can maintain their credit scores and still access the financial resources that they need. This prudent idea not only contributes to retaining a good credit rating but also equips people with sufficient knowledge to make the right choices that resonate with their financial goals.

Keeping Old Accounts Open

Having open lines of credit, especially long-term established ones, is an important component of keeping a healthy credit profile. The rationale behind the decision to retain old accounts can be seen in terms of the various advantages that it provides. These will add to the credit history length, which forms a significant part of a credit score. Account age is one of the tests that proves to have experience and reliability over time. Therefore, a long-standing account increases the average age of credit lines, which is a positive signal to lenders that evaluate creditworthiness.

In addition, old accounts act as a buffer to credit use ratios. The usage rate is the proportion of the credit that is being used. Holding older accounts open results in an increase in the total available credit and, therefore, could reduce the utilization ratio should balances remain constant or fall. This is one of the most vital ratios in credit scoring models, and it is generally recommended to keep the ratio at less than 30% to score best.

Sealing old accounts may cause the unintended result of using more credit, particularly when there is a balance in the remaining accounts. Such a change sends a false message to creditors that the company relies more on credit than it really does. Furthermore, it is possible to lower the total credit limit by closing an account, which can be more difficult to control in terms of its use.

In addition to the mechanical component of credit scoring, there is also a psychological and strategic component to maintaining accounts open. Access to a larger credit limit may also mean financial flexibility in times of need without always having to request new credit. This may prove particularly helpful in unexpected situations, like unexpected costs or interim cash flow problems, where a buffer may avoid the resort to high-interest borrowing solutions like payday loans.

These accounts should be managed, though. They can be kept open by monitoring regularly and using old credit accounts occasionally, after which they will not be closed as a result of inactivity. Other issuers of credit cards might shut down accounts that are not used much in the long term, nullifying the benefits of holding them. Thus, these accounts can be kept alive by making small purchases periodically, which are paid for in the near future.

Moreover, it is generally beneficial to leave old accounts open, but that is not without its traps. Consumers need to be aware of any annual maintenance charges on some credit cards. When the benefits are not worth the cost of maintaining the account open, then it might be worth considering an alternative, including negotiating a fee waiver or moving to a no-fee card.

Finally, the decision to retain open old accounts must be a component of a larger, strategic credit management approach. It is the trade-off between the advantages of long credit history and low utilization, and the realities of individual financial behavior and objectives. When meticulously managed, such accounts can serve individuals as a tool towards enhancing their credit report and financial health.

Avoiding Common Pitfalls

Credit is a complicated business and one that may present a lot of difficulty to someone fresh in dealing with it or trying to recover. Among the greatest obstacles is the number of fallacies and pitfalls that can doom even the most careful credit user. Being protective of your financial health is the first step, and that starts with the realization of the following traps.

One of the most common mistakes is that one must have a balance on their credit cards in order to establish credit. This myth has been known to lead to unwarranted payment of interest and can delay financial growth. The truth is that it is more advantageous to clear balances at the end of every month since this reflects good financial habits and maintains the credit utilization quotient at a low point, a key requirement in credit scoring.

The other pitfall is the lure of quick fixes, which are usually sold as magic cures to credit problems. They include services that offer quick credit score improvement or so-called credit sweeps, which purport to purge negative items from reports. These kinds of offers are usually too good to be considered true and may prove to be more economically destructive. Sustainable credit and legal improvement is a slow and continuous process; no quick way to real improvement.

One more concern is credit repair scams. Such scams include companies that require payment of advance fees, promise of guaranteed results, or claim to be able to remove accurate negative information on credit reports. They should question such promises and instead seek the services of reputable credit counseling. It is important to know that the real process of credit repair includes challenging erroneous information in credit reports and, over time, building better financial habits.

Another pitfall to avoid is the effect of applying for excess credit within a short time. Multiple tough inquiries within a short period may reduce credit scores and raise a red flag to potential lenders. It is better to combine credit applications in time and apply only when you need it, as every application has to be planned and productive in the long run.

Additionally, most people make the mistake of closing old credit accounts in the belief that this is a wise thing to do. However, older accounts make the credit history longer, and this attribute is a vital factor in credit scoring systems. It is usually more prudent to leave accounts open with a little or no balance than to close them and have a healthy length of credit history.

Another frequent problem is the lack of understanding of the role that credit monitoring plays. Monitoring services offer a great deal of information about credit activity, but they are not an alternative to proactive credit management. These tools should be used to ensure that consumers remain aware of their credit situation, but they must also participate in activities that will enhance their credit health.

Finally, one cannot become a credit manager without the emotional component. The tension and anxiety that come with credit problems can give rise to impulsive actions that are harmful to long-term financial well-being. Credit management should be handled with care and a defined plan of action, and one should take it step by step to make things better instead of trying to correct everything instantly. It takes time, effort, and sometimes the desire to consult with some trusted financial advisors to build a good credit profile.

Being aware of these pitfalls and learning to avoid them will help people navigate credit management issues more effectively, resulting in a more stable financial position and increased opportunities in the future.

6

HANDLING CREDIT SETBACKS

Rebuilding After Bankruptcy

It is not an easy task, and once a person has gone through bankruptcy, the path towards financial stability might appear discouraging. However, with careful planning and time, the credit can be restored successfully. First, it is important to learn about the effect of bankruptcy on credit reports and credit ratings. A bankruptcy can substantially lower a credit score and remain on a credit report for as long as ten years, depending on the type of bankruptcy, Chapter 7 or Chapter 13. Nevertheless, this does not mean that you should be defeated.

The first year of the bankruptcy is to be devoted to the attainment of financial stability and the establishment of basic accounts. This is a time to establish a firm credit base for the future. Credit cards and credit-builder loans are necessary at this stage. These financial instruments demand a deposit, or security, which lowers the risk to those providing these loans, but also enables individuals to prove that they can use these credits responsibly.

Another important step to prevent further delayed payments, which would be counterproductive to recovery, is to automate payments. Automation of utility payments, rent, and any secured credit products will make sure that bills are paid as they become due, and will help to restore a positive history of payment. It is also recommended that one should have a low credit utilization ratio by ensuring that balances are kept well below the credit limit on any revolving accounts.

At the start of the second year, it is possible to shift attention a bit toward developing better credit habits and gradually creating a stronger credit profile. It can be a smart move to apply to a credit union in your area to get a credit-builder loan. Such institutions tend to have good rates and are less reluctant to deal with people who are reestablishing their credit. It is also time to begin taking close care of the credit report and making sure that all the details are current and correct.

Between the years three and five, it should be possible to see gradual improvements. Having steady payment and credit management will begin to pay off during this period. It is also the moment to consider adding credit by using new credit lines carefully, however, only when necessary and after careful consideration of conditions and consequences on the credit rating.

During this recovery process, it is important to communicate clearly with the future creditors or landlords. A chance to explain the situation of bankruptcy will help reduce the negative attitudes towards it. Written explanations or scripts and templates of these discussions can give people the strength to defend themselves.

In the end, credit restoration in the wake of bankruptcy is a process of perseverance and wise choices. Following a systematic strategy, relying on the tools of financial management available, and being disciplined in their financial management habits, people can work step-by-step to rebuild their creditworthiness and recover financial stability.

Overcoming Divorce-Related Challenges

Divorce is a life-changing issue that can have significant economic impacts on an individual, particularly their credit situation. A variety of issues can be described as typical of this stage, as people have to grapple with the issue of untangling the financial commitments they made jointly and establishing new and separate credit histories.

Managing joint accounts is one of the most significant challenges in this transition, and it can create financial turbulence if the issue is not resolved soon. One of the issues that is usually overlooked in the intense emotional turmoil that is the divorce process is the joint credit cards and loans, which grow as a result of missed payments and added debt when the communication forms are not met, and either party does not take responsibility. People must also learn to separate or shut down joint accounts as soon as possible so that any remaining balances can be effectively divided, so that there will be no misunderstandings and financial stress.

To successfully distance themselves, the first thing people should do is to eliminate authorized user statuses and joint accounts. The latter is usually done by informing creditors of the legal separation or divorce, so that everyone knows about the financial liability changes. Another important thing is to update the personal information with credit bureaus; this will help avoid any future confusion of credit and also make sure that the current credit report is accurate and in line with the current state of the individual.

Another major issue that comes up during the settlement of divorce is negotiating the debt responsibility. Close collaboration with attorneys is necessary in order to clarify payment responsibilities. This can stop disagreements and make sure that the debts are solved, rather than not. It is a good idea to request the creditors' written confirmation concerning the status of the credit account and any amendments to it, as it can serve as a safety net, providing evidence of the agreed-upon terms and conditions.

With people becoming financially independent after the divorce, credit health is an issue that should be considered. The first step to a new credit identity is to open individual credit cards or loans in your name. This shows not just financial stability but is also useful in establishing a good credit history. It is also necessary to monitor the credit reports of the activity or the mistake of a former partner, since the goal is to safeguard the image of the financial institution and prevent a potential confrontation.

In addition, the impact of divorce, in terms of emotion, cannot be overestimated. Financial uncertainty is a stressful challenge that may be impossible to overcome, but taking a tactical approach to credit management may help reduce some of the pressure. A budget, realistic financial objectives, and professional financial advice can help to give a clear picture and direction through this difficult period.

It is important not only to manage current obligations to rebuild credit after divorce but also to develop habits to promote long-term financial health. Frequent and punctual payments and low credit utilization are some major habits that can boost credit scores in the long run. Credit surveillance services might help to get some clues concerning the financial track and avoid troubles.

Although it may seem like a long and winding journey to economic salvation after divorce, it is also a chance to embark on self-development and economic empowerment. People can achieve a solid base to lead a secure and steady financial future by taking measures to handle credit problems proactively. It is not only about clearing an obstacle that can be present today, but it also includes a lifetime of prudent and responsible money management.

Recovery from Job Loss

The sudden change in employment may be as shocking as an earthquake to both personal finances and mood. Such a two-fold influence requires a strategic response to immediate financial triage and longer-term credit recovery. In the case of an abrupt loss of income, one must, at a minimum, accept the seriousness of the situation and the consequences it can cause on a credit report. This awareness prepares the groundwork for taking initiative.

The process of communication becomes one of the pillars in the aftermath. Early contact with creditors to discuss the situation may allow access to a range of relief programs like deferrals of payments, forbearance, or access to hardship programs.

Various organizations will be happy to cooperate with people who show an active approach to fulfilling their financial part of the bailout in times of trouble.

At the same time, it is important to prioritize costs and build a new budget that corresponds to the new financial reality. The budget must be based on critical areas and also on areas where costs can be reduced. Having a reminder system of due dates means that, despite limited funds, it is possible to prevent missed payments that also worsen credit scores.

Once the income level becomes stable, either with new employment or otherwise, credit restoration should become one of the priorities. This can begin with little, easy-to-handle measures like getting a secured credit card. These credit cards are supported by a cash deposit, which provides one with an opportunity to show that he/she can use the credit responsibly, without risking falling into more debt. On-time credit payments on such accounts can also help to increase credit scores in the long run.

Furthermore, credit monitoring tools may be used to provide effective information regarding the status of an individual's credit, and thus, help monitor the progress and identify potential mistakes that may occur during this transitional phase. Consistency in checking credit reports is important as errors are quickly disputed and corrected before they cause undue harm to credit scores.

It may also be motivating to share personal experiences of resilience and recovery. We might take the example of Andre, who was laid off. Still, he was able to recover and concentrate on his skills and networking, managing to obtain a job that not only earned him income again but also provided him with better prospects. His experience highlights the need to have a healthy attitude and use the resources at hand to survive during times of unemployment.

The bottom line is that job loss recovery is a complex process that requires a mix of financial management in the short term and credit reconstruction in the long term. It takes time, discipline, and readiness to seek assistance and guidance when necessary. Following such measures would allow people to use what might initially appear as an insurmountable setback as a chance to renew and grow in terms of finances.

Addressing Identity Theft

The issue of identity theft is rampant and has been known to leave millions of people with derailed lives, in addition to capriciously triggering heavy financial losses. In a situation where identity theft is discovered, the first actions undertaken might be critical in reducing the damage and preparing the ground for recovery. The first step is to issue a fraud alert to all three major credit bureaus, Experian, Equifax, and TransUnion. This warning is a notice to creditors that they need to go the extra mile in confirming the identity of whoever is trying to open accounts in your name. It serves as a deterrent as well as a reminder to the creditors that your data can be stolen.

At the same time, reporting through IdentityTheft.gov to the Federal Trade Commission (FTC) gives you an official history of the theft and produces a recovery action plan that best suits your circumstances. This report will play a critical role since it will not only record the incident but also help prove it against fraudulent charges. Also, reporting to the police will help further substantiate your case. It will ultimately provide a local law enforcement record that creditors or credit bureaus may need when the dispute arises.

Another important thing to do is to secure your financial accounts. This will include calling banks and credit card issuers to report the fraudulent activity. Accounts that have been manipulated or opened with bad intentions should be closed or frozen so that additional unauthorized transactions cannot occur. Most institutions have their own fraud departments, and they can guide and support you through the process here.

In instances where instant operations are regulated, one will need to initiate a fight with credit bureaus to wipe fraud accounts off. This means that you will send a copy of the letter to all the bureaus, with a copy of your FTC report and any other supporting documentation, e.g., evidence of identity and a police report. The use of templates can simplify this, and all the information required is included and well presented.

Vigilance is the key factor in the post-identity theft period. Another way you can stay alert to any additional fraud attempts is by establishing continuous credit monitoring services. These types of services will typically inform you of new inquiries or accounts, so that when there is any suspicion, you can act immediately.

Having a personal identity theft recovery log can be a useful tool to keep track of developments and make a record of communications with creditors, credit bureaus, and law enforcement. This kind of journal can serve as a reference in future disputes or inquiries, in order to obtain a complete record of all measures that have been taken.

Along with these practical measures, credibility takes time to regain momentum. However, with time, when fake accounts are deleted and your credit report is fixed, steps toward identity protection are part of financial well-being. These include the utilization of two-factor authentication for sensitive accounts, changing passwords regularly, and being cautious about sharing personal information.

Finally, the challenge of correcting the damage of identity theft does not only center on the correction of earlier damages but also on the development of a durable mechanism to prevent future attacks. You can control your credit and have a more secure financial future by learning what to do and taking the necessary steps to protect your credit.

7

LEGAL RIGHTS AND PROTECTIONS

Fair Credit Reporting Act

The Fair Credit Reporting Act (FCRA) is one of the pillars of consumer rights that creates a veil of protection and is projected to ensure fairness, accuracy, and privacy of credit information use. In its simplest essence, the FCRA provides individuals the right to a free annual credit report from each of the major credit bureaus, Experian, Equifax, and TransUnion. This not only enhances transparency but also empowers consumers to remain aware of their financial health and take proactive measures to maintain their credit health.

Key to the FCRA is the right to challenge inaccuracies. In case a consumer notices any mistaken entries, be it through clerical mistakes, identity theft, or other causes, they can dispute such errors. To correct the evils, the act requires the credit bureaus to carry out investigations on such conflicts within a specific time, say 30 days, in order that it can correct the evils in good time. This practice shows that one should be observant and advise consumers to look at their credit report regularly to help correct mistakes that could adversely affect their credit rating.

In addition to correcting errors, the FCRA gives the right to request unverifiable information to be removed. This implies that if a credit bureau fails to validate an entry on a consumer's report, the entry should be removed. These play a critical role in maintaining the credit profile integrity of a consumer, as only verifiable and accurate information is utilized during credit appraisal.

The act also restricts who is authorized to access a consumer credit report. In most cases, access is only provided to entities that have a legitimate need, like lenders, insurers, employers (with consent), and landlords. This restriction helps in guarding personal financial data; therefore, any third party would not see sensitive data.

The FCRA in practice gives consumers the ability to emerge as the authors of their credit stories. One such case is where an individual falls victim to identity theft; the law allows them to place a warning about the fraud on their credit reports, that is, to warn potential creditors to exercise increased caution. Furthermore, the FCRA is beneficial to the consumer because it provides templates and instructions for composing dispute letters and requests to delete information, which facilitates the enforcement of consumer rights.

However, one should be aware of the scope of the FCRA. Although it does provide strong protection, it does not remove factual negative information on a credit report. Late payments or bankruptcies result in negative entries that have been specified to be reported in seven years (most delinquencies) or bankruptcies, which are reported over a period of ten years. Learning these boundaries will assist in establishing reasonable goals in credit repair.

Essentially, FCRA is not a simple kind of law, but an enabling instrument. Consumers can sift through credit reporting complexities with ease, as it has translated its provisions into actionable steps. Whether it is challenging a stranger's account or guaranteeing that only trusted individuals can access their credit records, the FCRA offers a benchmark in developing and maintaining a healthy credit profile. Due to awareness and active participation, people can also leverage the act to their financial benefit and make sound decisions based on their financial and personal goals.

Fair Debt Collection Practices

The world of debt is overwhelming, and when paired with assertive debt-collector tactics, it can be not easy to navigate. The awareness of the Fair Debt Collection Practices Act (FDCPA) is justified when consumers prefer to protect themselves against unjust practices. This federal legislation gives very clear guidelines on what debt collectors can and cannot do, and also gives guidelines to give a feel of fairness and openness.

The ban on abusive practices is one of the central provisions of the FDCPA. Debt collectors are also instructed not to harass or threaten. This is not limited to using obscene language, making numerous phone calls to annoy, or even threatening to use violence. This knowledge of such boundaries will give consumers the power to realize when a collector is crossing the line and to act accordingly.

In addition, the act provides that debt collectors should not violate the privacy and convenience of the consumer. Unreasonable hours are not allowed, i.e., prior to 8 a.m. or after 9 p.m., except at the request of the consumer. This feature helps the consumer maintain the illusion of normalcy and control their own time, without overbearing communication.

Another important protection provided by the FDCPA is the right to validation of the debt. On demand, collectors are required to send written confirmation of the debt, including details about the amount due and the name of the original creditor. This is required to assist in ensuring that they are not taken by surprise by debts that they do not owe or by debts that were misreported. In the event that a consumer challenges the debt within 30 days after the original communication, then the collector shall not attempt to collect the debt until the debt is established.

The act also covers the matter of false or misleading representations. Debt collectors are not allowed to misrepresent the value, legality, or character of any debt.

They are not allowed to suggest that failure to pay will lead to arrest and prosecution, which is not really contemplated. With knowledge about these prohibitions, consumers would be able to identify and report false practices.

The FDCPA provides an avenue of complaint to people who have chronic issues with debt collectors. Consumers are able to record violations and file them with the Federal Trade Commission (FTC) or with the Consumer Financial Protection Bureau (CFPB). A detailed record of all contacts with debt collectors (dates, times, and a summary of what was said) may prove invaluable to back up a complaint.

In addition, the FDCPA allows consumers to sue collectors who flout the act. In the event of victory, customers can be reimbursed for their losses and lawyer costs, which can not only protect them but also act as a deterrent to future abuse.

Knowledge and use of the safeguards of the FDCPA can dramatically shift the consumer-debt collector power dynamic. It provides people with skills to defend their rights so that their relationships with collectors can be carried out within the law. This provides the consumers with greater assurance and knowledge of how to tackle the issues that the collection of the debts poses; it demystifies the debt and therefore their own financial wellness and tranquility.

State-Specific Laws

Credit repair can be tricky when one does not have a clear grasp of the different legal systems that are in place in different states. The rights and duties that consumers are entitled to can vary greatly, and it is important to understand how state laws can support or prevent the credit repair process. Federal laws are thought to be a minimum of consumer rights, but in many cases, state-specific laws will add an extra level of security or difficulty.

State laws can be instrumental in one aspect: the statute of limitations on debt. This is the period of time during which a creditor is legally allowed to take legal action against a debtor to recover a debt. These time limits differ by state, with some states having shorter limits, which may help consumers by shortening the time they are legally at risk of becoming targets of the collection lawsuit. To provide an example, a state such as California may have a written contract with a four-year statute of limitations, whereas Texas may provide a different time frame. Consumers interested in taking advantage of legal protections must understand these differences to do so.

The other important consideration is the protection of wage garnishment. Other states provide more consumer-friendly protections and the amount or nature of the income that can be garnished. One example is a state such as North Carolina or South Carolina, which has a law protecting wages against garnishment of most debts other than child support and taxes. Such protections can have a considerable impact on an individual's financial stability, particularly in the context of aggressive debt collection practices.

Another area that may have state differences is medical debt. With medical bills being unique debts, some states have passed legislation to offer extra protection to consumers who are challenged by the debt. Such laws may contain clauses such as caps on interest rates charged on medical expenses or provide longer periods of repayment to reduce the financial burden on the consumer.

Conversely, some state laws may create a challenge to credit repair. On the indicative side, certain states permit certain types of debts to be reported on credit reports over extended periods relative to the federal rule, and, consequently, it is difficult to clean up the individual credit report. State rules also exist, however, of what might be termed renewing of judgment that may extend the lapsing date of a debt, which may complicate escaping past financial conditions.

In order to overcome these complexities, consumers need to conduct extensive research and make use of resources at their disposal. State attorney general websites and state-specific consumer protection offices can be invaluable resources in learning about local regulations and laws. Such resources can help consumers harness the legal resources they have at their disposal so that they are not just aware of their rights, but also know how to exercise them.

In addition, it is important to have an idea of how state laws apply to real-life cases. To illustrate the point, the same scenario can unfold in radically different ways based on the state, so that California and Texas approach the issue of medical debt differently and generate different outcomes due to the same case. Equally, the statute of limitations concerning credit card debt in New York and Florida could vary, which could affect how consumers resolve such debt.

Altogether, state-specific legislations provide powerful credit repair options, though these legislations should also be treated with a grain of salt. This is because the consumer will be in a better position to be more defensive of his rights and will be more tactical in his credit repair efforts after knowing the provisions of such laws.

When to Seek Legal Help

When it comes to the intricacies of credit management, there are times when it is not only prudent to consult legal help, but it is also necessary. It can be the knowledge of the particular circumstances under which the law needs to be applied that enables individuals to protect their rights and even to alleviate financial hardship.

The most common cases in which an individual may require legal assistance include when one is sued on an already settled debt. In this type of situation, a lawyer can be of invaluable aid, be it in establishing the fact that the debt was paid, or that the claim was invalid, or by bargaining for a settlement. Legal education can be relevant in passing the court process without violating the rights and presenting all the needed documents properly.

The other emergency occurs when a creditor or debt collector continuously breaches the Fair Debt Collection Practices Act (FDCPA) even after being informed of his/her actions. This is a federal statute that gives the consumer rights against unfair practices, and an attorney can assist them in enforcing those rights and possibly win damages against the consumer. Lawyers may assist in documenting the breaches, launching a complaint, and potentially pursuing litigation.

Another case in which legal assistance could be offered is the issue of zombie debts or debts that are past the statute of limitations. After a time-barred debt has elapsed, this debt cannot be collected in court. Nevertheless, aggressive collection efforts may still be directed at the consumers. A lawyer can explain the status of those debts, prevent an illegal attempt at collection, and provide advice on communicating with collectors.

In addition, it is important to be aware of the statute of limitations for consumer debts. The length of this legal period depends on the state and determines the maximum time a creditor has to bring a lawsuit to recover a debt. An attorney can assist in establishing a time-barred debt and provide recommendations as to how to proceed, e.g., a cease-and-desist letter to collectors.

Having a lawyer on board is also invaluable in addressing matters concerning debt re-ageing--the ploy of having collectors re-age old debts as per the illegitimate purpose of increasing their apparent value collectability. A lawyer can help consumers challenge such unfair practices so that their credit report shows appropriate, legal information.

Moreover, a consumer can be in a situation where they require legal assistance when making a complaint to a consumer protection organization such as the Consumer Financial Protection Bureau (CFPB) or the Federal Trade Commission (FTC). These agencies can step into disputes that have not been resolved yet, or where there exists negative harassment, and where legal advice would be more effective, complete, and finalize the complaints.

Overall, although numerous problems related to credit may be addressed without the assistance of a lawyer, there are situations when the help of a legal specialist is not only useful but indispensable. Knowledge of the necessity of hiring an attorney can save more money and can rescue rights and peace of mind in the credit management world, which is sometimes a shambles.

8

AVOIDING SCAMS AND PREDATORY PRACTICES

Recognizing Credit Repair Scams

The credit repair market is quite tricky to navigate since it is saturated with promises of quick-fix solutions and miracle fixes. Unluckily, this atmosphere is conducive to disingenuousness, as it targets people who are in dire need of raising their economic status. It is important to be aware of these frauds to avoid losing money and becoming emotionally disturbed.

Another most obvious indicator of a credit repair scam is the initial request for money prior to service delivery. There exists a legitimate credit repair company whose services are legally obligatory to be offered even before payment is given. When a service demands payment before any work is completed, it is a huge red flag that it may be a fraud. Likewise, when promises are made of instant or guaranteed results, it is usually too good to be true. Repairing credit takes time, patience, and follow-up of legal procedures, and no effective service can promise immediate results.

The other trick that most fraudsters apply is the assurance to delete genuine negative credit report contents. Errors can be challenged and deleted, but correct information, no matter how bad it is, cannot be deleted from records in a court of law. Any claims to the opposite are misleading and illegal most of the time. Also, no written contract or necessary disclosures are another indication of a scam. Legitimate services will offer a written contract that defines the number of services to be rendered and terms of the engagement as required by the Credit Repair Organizations Act.

Fraudsters usually use psychological techniques to gain trust and force victims to make rash judgments. The use of high-pressure sales tactics, urgent time offers, etc., is aimed at creating a sense of urgency. They can apply official-sounding seals, legal jargon, or insider language in a way that makes it sound authoritative and credible. These tricks are to disorient and intimidate people into submission.

The only way to avoid such scams is to do extensive research and to ensure that a credit repair business is legitimate. Complaints with the Better Business Bureau or the Consumer Financial Protection Bureau can help to understand the legitimacy of a company. Another important step is to confirm state licensing (where applicable). Particular questions, including how the service will enhance your credit and asking that the contract be written, are a good way of evaluating the validity of the offer.

Along with these measures, it is important to build an attitude of doubt and perseverance. The safest way of improving credit is not to take shortcuts, but to make gradual, legal strides towards better credit. Membership in respectable support circles can provide counsel and experience, as well as affirm the need to exercise due diligence and sound judgment in decision-making.

The bottom line is that the most effective defense against credit repair scams is empowerment with knowledge and resources. By understanding the red flags and the legal environment, they can protect themselves against fraud and work to achieve an authentic credit improvement.

Dodging Predatory Offers

Within the expansive forest of credit management, there is a perilous land full of predatory deals that prey on the weak. This is done under the guise of help in order to get people into the deep waters of financial schemes they would not have gotten into under other guise of help. The key to this kind of trickery is understanding how to stay financially healthy and not fall into the traps that can trap even the wariest consumer.

Most predatory financial products target those with poor credit and offer them solutions that seem like lifelines, and in the end, end up trapping them in debt. The examples of Payday loans are normally packaged as solutions to financial crises. The loans are highly promoted in low-income residential areas, where the financial stability of low-income earners is assured without having to undergo a credit check. The high interest rates charged, however, tend to plunge borrowers into an endless debt trap that they can hardly come out of.

In the same vein, rent-to-own and tradeline packages are marketed as a way to own or to get a better credit score. These deals may be tempting to people who have no access to traditional sources of credit. Though rent-to-own contracts claim to give the consumer possession of goods after a sequence of payments, it is common to see a consumer pay much more than the market value of the item. Tradeline packages, or piggybacking on another individual's credit account in order to improve one's credit score, are sometimes a cause of legal issues unless handled correctly.

A second fraudulent service is known as Credit Profile Numbers (CPNs), and is sold as a means of obtaining a new credit identity. However, they might appear to be a clean slate, the use of a CPN can cause legal complications, especially when it comes to the use of a fake Social Security Number. Financial and legal risks often outweigh the facts behind all these promises of quick results and new starts.

In order to defend against these predatory traps, one must develop a sense of great skepticism and a culture of conducting extensive research. An evaluation of the offer must start with a gut check, or a moment to doubt the validity and need of the offer. This includes online review and complaint search, communication with nonprofit credit counselors, and assessment of the offer in relation to more traditional, proven financial solutions.

The testimonials of the lives of people who have managed to escape the predatory offers are the ones that work best in real life. One such case was a reader who, despite first finding a CPN offer appealing, chose to go about legally raising his credit score, thus becoming financially stable. The other narrative could be that of someone who found himself in the payday loan trap, and negotiated terms of payment with their creditors, and as such, they could now use their money as they wanted.

It takes alertness and teaching to avoid being caught in predatory offers. People can protect their credit by learning the tactics that are likely to be employed to take advantage of those who are in dire financial situations and by focusing on making well-informed choices. The road to financial empowerment is one where we make informed decisions, and every decision taken carefully and judiciously is a step towards a safe and sound financial future.

Protecting Yourself Online

In the era of the Internet, online vigilance is the only way to ensure the security of your credit data. This is based on the premise that, when it comes to safeguarding your online presence, the first step should be to practice strong password management. Use complex, unique passwords, one password per financial account, and the chances of unauthorized access would significantly decrease. A password manager can help make this process easier so that you never use the same password again or use easily guessable combinations.

Another important step is to improve your security environment by using two-factor authentication (2FA). Not only does this additional level of verification demand a password, but it also demands a second type of verification, dramatically increasing the difficulty with which cybercriminals can crack into your accounts. Use 2FA as much as you can, particularly on sites sensitive to credit checks or money.

Be cautious of phishing, which is usually conveyed in the format of emails and messages that seem to be sent by a reputable financial organization. These messages can deceive you into sharing any personal information. Never ignore URLs with some minor cases of misspelling or even extra characters that are signs of a suspicious site. In addition, do not click on doubtful links and do not download attachments from unknown authors.

Free Wi-Fi is very convenient, but it is also a great threat to your credit. These networks are not very secure, and therefore, hackers can easily intercept data. One should not use financial accounts or enter personal details when using free Wi-Fi. When you are forced to use such networks, you should use a virtual private network (VPN) that will encrypt your internet connection and secure your data.

Speaking of sensitive documents, it is important to consider security and leverage encrypted file-sharing services when sharing them online. These services provide confidentiality to your documents as they are being transferred. Do not use unsecured mail to send Social Security numbers or any other sensitive information that malicious parties can hack.

It is important to create a digital credit hygiene routine. Periodically (once every month or quarter), check your online security settings. This will involve ensuring that they have permission to access the applications and account access history, as well as replacing their passwords on a regular basis, which are among the measures used to eradicate the risks of an intrusion. It is also advisable to ensure that your devices are up to date with the most recent security patches, which will help mitigate any vulnerabilities that hackers can use.

When you think you have fallen prey to a scam, move quickly. Say goodbye to the scammer and discontinue payments. Ensure that you change passwords to your financial accounts and monitor the accounts against fraudulent transactions. File a complaint with the appropriate authorities, including the Federal Trade Commission

(FTC) or the Consumer Financial Protection Bureau (CFPB), and ask the major credit bureaus to put a fraud alert on your file.

These steps will help you avert credit fraud and stay safe online by making them a habit in your daily routine. You are already aware of the security threats that are present and are still upgrading your strategies to defend your financial health in the online space.

Building a Support Network

The role of community and support cannot be underestimated in the field of credit repair and financial management. Networking with other like-minded people can go a long way in enhancing credit improvement and protection efforts. This mass knowledge is available on several online and offline platforms, where people can share tips and stories of success and provide support.

Social media groups and online forums are the newfound meeting places where people come together to share their credit experience. Facebook and other platforms, such as Reddit, have many credit repair groups where members share and discuss strategies and experiences and provide support to each other. These online communities provide a treasure trove of knowledge, including practical guidance on how to counteract mistakes made and offering emotional solace in times of defeat. However, they also need to belong to well-managed groups with clear guidelines to support a safe and constructive environment.

Reputable organizations also provide peer support, professional guidance, and resources to manage credit. An example of nonprofit credit counseling and other legal aid institutions is the National Foundation for Credit Counseling (NFCC) and local Legal Aid offices. These organizations are priceless resources to those who require organized assistance and professional counselling on how to resolve their difficult credit problems.

One must be careful and discerning when dealing with any community or service. Strict rules and active moderation of community groups are recommended to prevent toxic communities or scams. It is also wise to avoid organizations that promote products or even demand money to join. With the selection of appropriate communities, people have a chance to get real support instead of becoming victims of predatory activity.

In addition to professional and peer support, accountability and motivation can be encouraged by using the support of trusted friends and family in the credit improvement process. Constituting a schedule of check-ins or establishing a credit buddy arrangement with loved ones may offer the motivation one needs to continue to stay on track. Exchanging progress charts or celebrating milestones collectively can make what can be a lonely process of credit repair a collaborative effort.

The construction of a support network is concerned not only with getting assistance but also with returning it. Personal experiences and insights can be enhanced by sharing with other people on the same journey, which leads to a cyclical reinforcement cycle. It can help them join and become active participants in such communities, and it can help them develop a culture of support and resilience. The credit improvement process is turned into a community project.

Stated, a support network can be viewed as a source of strength in its quest to repair its credit and achieve financial stability. Online forums, professional counseling, or personal relationships can all play a role in determining whether one feels overwhelmed or empowered financially due to the encouragement and advice of a community. The aid and guidance of others can help clarify the way as people navigate the wires and machinations of credit management, and it can turn the problems into chances to advance and prosper.

9

MAINTAINING LONG-TERM CREDIT HEALTH

Regular Credit Check-Ups

Credit checks are a habit that is crucial to staying financially healthy. It is just as important to check your credit status as it is to check your physical health regularly, in order to stay financially stable and avoid unplanned problems. Habit is a procedural method of checking credit reports and credit scores with a view to understanding their financial position, irregularities, and coming up with sound decisions on how to use credit.

Regular credit checks enable people to keep track of their credit rating, which is an imperative part of their financial identity. A credit score can affect many things in life, including obtaining a mortgage, getting a car loan, or even the interest charged on credit cards. With information about the problems affecting credit scores, individuals can actively make efforts to improve and maintain their scores high to enjoy better financial opportunities in the future.

The early detection and correction of errors or fraudulent activities is one of the best advantages of regular credit check-ups. There are also some errors that credit reports may include, like poor account history or identity theft, which may lead to poor credit scores. Checking credit reports regularly would help to identify such mistakes on time and challenge the credit bureaus to rectify the records.

In addition to this, the management of debts and the knowledge of spending patterns are helped by frequent observation of credit. It enables people to observe the impact of their financial habits, including their payment history and credit utilization, on their credit scores. This information encourages better money habits, such as paying bills when they are due and keeping a small balance on the credit card, which are essential for a healthy credit score.

The development of a credit check-up habit assumes the identification of specific intervals for credit checks and credit report examination. Individuals may wish to view their credit every month, taking advantage of free online sites, or some may wish to view their credit once per quarter or once per year to have a detailed view of their credit report. In addition to these reviews, credit monitoring services can also be included to provide notification of any important changes, such as the opening of a new account, a hard inquiry, etc., which can also prevent the possibility of identity theft.

It can be said that technology can also be used to enhance the credit check-up process, along with an individual's watch. Numerous sites and applications are free to monitor credit scores and to access credit reports, and this has made monitoring credit health easier than ever before. The functions often contained in these applications include budgeting and specific guidance on how to optimize their credit, which enables them to make good financial decisions.

In order to maximize the regular credit checks, they need to be able to set physical goals in terms of the credit scores. Setting specific objectives may motivate individuals to adhere to regular monitoring and take all the right steps to ensure they achieve a specific level of score in the credit history by either pursuing the goal of finding a loan with more favorable terms or pursuing the goal of reaching a specific level of score in the credit history.

Finally, frequent credit checks are preventive steps that will eventually guide such individuals to manage their finances. They will be in a position to maintain their credit, be aware of any trap that could befall them, and be in a position to place themselves so that they can be economically prosperous. This is not just to help them plan the already existing financial demands, but also to help them be prepared in case they can get opportunities in the future and have a stable and safe financial orientation.

Celebrating Milestones

Making serious strides in controlling personal credit is an admirable achievement, and it can be characterized by a sequence of milestones that are worth celebration. Each milestone is not only a step towards financial freedom but also an acknowledgment of the rigor and stamina it took to wade through the intricacies of credit management. These celebrations, be it by achieving a new credit rating or negotiating a low-interest rate, are a chance to see the journey and the tricks that have carried you to this point.

The achievement of a certain credit score is one of the first things a significant number of individuals celebrate. It could be 650, 700, and beyond, based on where one begins and the goals one has in terms of finances. These accomplishments are mostly achieved after working hard to pay off on time, cut down on accumulated debts, and properly use credit facilities. The gratification of getting a higher credit score is a strong incentive, effective in supporting positive financial habits and drawing a person further into devoting themselves to upholding or advancing a credit score.

The other milestone is a successful negotiation of more favorable terms on existing credit accounts. This may include getting a better interest rate on a credit card or getting a larger credit limit, both of which can make a big difference in personal financial status. A decrease in the overall cost of borrowing with lower interest rates and an increase in credit limits with a healthier credit profile. The celebration of such milestones, in addition to individual financial progress, also underlines the importance of being active in the management of accounts and communication with creditors.

In addition to these quantitative milestones, qualitative milestones are also an important aspect of the credit management process. To take an example, when a person is able to read a credit report and actually comprehends what is in each section and how the financial status of the person is affected, then it is a huge achievement. This new knowledge gives people the power to control their credit stories and, therefore, allows them to identify mistakes, notice trends, and make better decisions regarding their future financial behavior.

These milestones may be celebrated in many different ways, representing both individual preferences and the importance of the accomplishment. Others might prefer to reward themselves with a little reward or experience, as a symbol of the progress achieved. Others would like to tell their success to friends or family and use these occasions to motivate and encourage others on the same path. The celebration, whatever the technique involved, is a strong reinforcing element of the positive behaviours and choices that resulted in the win.

Additionally, such festivals may serve as gateways, whereby one could evaluate their existing plans and amend them where needed. They can look back and see what has been a success and what might be done better, so they can establish new goals and keep moving. Such a cycle of goals, accomplishing them, and celebrating success creates a culture of development and resilience, both crucial to long-term financial success.

Finally, any commemoration of any milestone in credit management goes beyond recognition of progress. It is about appreciating the effort, hard work, and education it takes to get to these places. Step by step, as a result of appreciating every advance, people not only create a belief in their own capacity to handle their credit but also establish a foundation of financial well-being and liberation.

Staying Accountable

To achieve the goal of creating and sustaining a healthy credit profile, a system of accountability must be created. This will not only help in the attainment of the financial objectives but also inculcate a sense of responsibility and discipline. Establishing specific, concrete credit goals is one measure that works. They must be measurable, specific, and time-bound to track and evaluate. One such example is to meet a credit score of 700 within a year, with a target and time frame.

To facilitate these goals, it is useful to involve friends, family, or even social networks. It is possible to share progress with an appreciative group, and this can provide support and positive feedback to help the process seem less daunting. You can also find a lot of information and guidance through the online forums dedicated to credit improvement that are filled with people who have the same goals.

Accountability can be greatly boosted by developing visual tools (e.g., charts or logs). The tools remind one of one's progress at all times and could also help to identify which aspects should be improved. One such example could be a progress tracker, which tracks milestones, such as attaining a certain score or getting over an error.

In addition, one should celebrate even minor achievements so as to remain motivated. Any milestone reached, however minuscule it may be, should be celebrated. This may be as simple as a small snack or an outing, which reinforces the positive behavior and motivates further effort.

An accountability buddy can make a difference, too. This may be a friend or relative who knows your objectives and can check in with you on a regular basis. These meetings may be monthly or even once a fortnight, during which they can discuss mistakes, successes, and further actions.

In addition, personal stories and testimonials of success can be used to inspire and motivate others to follow the same path. To witness the struggle and the ultimate success of another person can bring hope and effective suggestions to overcome the hurdles.

One has to keep in mind that failures are an inherent part of the process. They are supposed to be regarded as learning experiences, but not failures. One of the very important ways of being accountable is to take a look back at what made the setback and how to prevent something identical from happening going forward.

To support this process, it can be incredibly helpful to visualize the achievements by using templates and trackers. Progress can be easily and regularly tracked through the use of printable or downloadable materials. These devices not only record the improvement but also serve as a reminder of the promises you have made to yourself in relation to financial health.

In summary, accountability in credit management would mean clear targets, supporting networks, visual aids, benchmark recognition, and learning from mistakes. With these practices becoming part of the routine, having a solid and stable credit profile can become a feasible and achievable outcome.

Continued Education and Vigilance

Any journey toward financial empowerment in the complex environment of credit management is a lifetime endeavor that comes with a commitment to additional education and consciousness. To navigate the complexities of credit health, it is necessary to be aware of not just the current rules and strategies but also the constantly changing environment of financial regulations and practices. People should also always be on the offensive with their attempts to safeguard and improve their credit scores.

Reviewing credit reports on a regular basis is considered one of the foundations of having good credit health. By doing this, individuals are kept up to date on their credit scores, and fraudulent activities or discrepancies are identified early. Reviewing credit reports issued by all three major bureaus, Experian, Equifax, and TransUnion, people can pay attention to the accuracy and up-to-date information presented in the credit reports. This is significant because any mistakes made in the credit report can result in a huge loss of money, e.g., inability to take a loan or high interest rates.

Now, besides checking the credit, it is also necessary to be aware of the new laws on credit and consumer rights. Other laws, such as the Fair Credit Reporting Act (FCRA) and the Fair Debt Collection Practices Act (FDCPA), enable a person to dispute wrongdoings and demand just or fair treatment from creditors and collectors. This is because knowing these rights allows them to speak up and prevent exploitation by the predatory behavior.

Another important part of financial literacy is education. Reading materials like workshops, online courses, and financial counseling can help you gain an understanding of the best credit management practices. These educational programs can guide people to realize the effect of using credit, why it is important to have different types of credit, and why it is good to pay the payments on time. Furthermore, they provide advice on how they should strategically apply to new credit without negatively impacting their credit rating.

Besides, the accountability culture and support culture could significantly enhance the credit journey. It can be motivated and learned together by building relationships with accountability partners or by participating in financial support groups. These networks give the chance to discuss the financial purpose, narrate the success story, and the experience of other people that positively influence habitual credit.

Another thing that should be noted is to be aware of scams and other fraudulent deals that are aimed at unaware consumers. There must be an understanding of the widespread scams, including credit repair frauds and phishing attacks. People must beware of deals that say they will fix their credit immediately or require you to make initial payments without any definite agreement. By being careful and suspicious of such offers, consumers will be able to shield themselves against financial losses.

Lastly, an effective credit plan is built on additional education and treatment. Individuals cannot just ensure their credit health stays healthy, but also become more financially independent and free by committing to a lifetime learning process and practicing active monitoring. One of the proactive measures that has been put in place to ensure they are in control of their financial future and that they make sound decisions that will help them in the long term is one of these.

10

CREDIT IN SPECIAL SITUATIONS

Military and Relocation Challenges

Military families have different kinds of problems to handle when it comes to credit and financial issues. Repeated relocations, deployments, and the vagaries of military life can cause a host of credit problems. Risk of missed payment due to delays in mail forwarding is one of the most common issues. When families change residence, they can forget about the bills and, as a result, pay them late and be charged with deposits and bad credit.

Another important obstacle is addressing changes. Whenever a military family moves, the family has to change its address with creditors, banks, and credit bureaus. Otherwise, they could get incorrect addresses on their credit report, which can cause a false identity or fraud alert. This is especially worrying since even minor mistakes could have far-reaching consequences on credit ratings, alongside impediments to getting new lines of credit.

The deployments bring on board another complexity. Soldiers could be posted in areas where few financial institutions are available and where it is difficult to pay and maintain accounts. Also, staying out of the home may lead to failure to maintain contact with creditors, another strain on the budget.

Luckily, military families can take some measures to alleviate these problems. Notifying credit bureaus of being a member of the Navy is one of the most important steps that will help avoid mistakes and new problems. Interest rate reduction and credit freezing in the face of active deployment are some of the benefits that the Servicemembers Civil Relief Act (SCRA) provides. This kind of action can provide much-needed financial relief and sanity.

Furthermore, there are military-family-specific resources that can help these families overcome such credit problems. They are guided and assisted by the Consumer Financial Protection Bureau (CFPB) and Military One Source agencies. Such institutes could contribute to correcting credit errors in the context of service provision and offer guidance to ease the financial burden.

In these credit problems, the emotional aspect cannot be understated. Shame, fear, or discouragement are normal feelings, but you must remember that credit does not make you or break you. It is important to develop a sense of resilience and stay positive. Any small wins and progress, however insignificant, should be celebrated as they help to increase morale and keep working to fix credit health.

It is also important to form a support network. Meeting other military families who are aware of the unique issues can help offer both emotional and practical help. It can be empowering to share experiences and strategies and create a community of resilience and mutual support.

Military life requires flexibility and strength, particularly in the area of finances. Military families can survive the challenges of frequent relocations and deployments by taking effective precautionary actions to correct any credit problems, using the resources available to them, and feeling positive about the difficulties they face. This commitment not only assists them in saving their future financially but also enhances their overall well-being in the face of uncertainties in life.

Handling Medical Debt

Medical debt is a difficult world to navigate without a plan and a good comprehension of the choices that exist. Unlike other types of debts, medical debt tends to come out of thin air and can accumulate rapidly because of the cost of healthcare. Such an obligation may weigh heavily on the financial well-being of an individual, impacting credit scores and future borrowing ability.

Management of medical debt should first begin by reviewing all medical bills and insurance statements to confirm that they are accurate. Billing mistakes are not unusual, and even minor mistakes may cause unnecessary costs. It is important to check that the services billed were actually received and that the charges are reasonable according to the terms of the insurance coverage. When there are discrepancies, the medical provider or the insurance company should be contacted, and the errors should be corrected as soon as possible.

After the debts have been verified, payment options need to be considered. Healthcare providers have plenty of payment arrangements where the patient can repay debt at a rate without interest. Such plans are negotiable directly with the provider's billing department. Also, there are financial assistance programs or charity care policies in some hospitals that lessen the amount due by a great deal in case of qualified persons.

The other strategy is negotiating settlements. The debt could be paid less than the amount due. This is possible through calling the billing office of the healthcare provider and offering a lump sum that is less than the debt. This usually works well during such negotiations, as the providers would rather receive something as opposed to nothing in case of default.

This may prove invaluable to medical debt consumers who have sunk neck deep into medical debt due to the professional services provided by a credit counselor or debt relief agency. These professionals will be able to develop a realistic budget, negotiate with suppliers, and provide financial health metrics. It is also important to mention that it is recommended to choose a reputable service, not to fall into a trap and waste more money.

One of the components of medical debt management is to monitor a credit report. Medical debts may be reflected on credit reports when they are sold to collection agencies, and this can have a devastating effect on credit scores. Periodically reviewing credit reports enables people to check the correctness of all information presented in the credit report and correct any anomalies in real time.

It is important to know the rights of the consumer in case the medical debt has already been referred to a collection agency. The Fair Debt Collection Practices Act (FDCPA) protects against the scamming behaviour of debt collectors, such as harassment or misrepresentation. They have the right to request that the debt be verified and any inaccuracy be disputed.

In some situations, when the medical burden is too big, bankruptcy may be a final option. Whereas bankruptcy may relieve people of debt, it also has long-term effects that are worth considering. By consulting a bankruptcy lawyer, they may be able to decide whether this is the right choice or not.

Finally, medical debt needs to be approached adequately and responsibly. Checking bills, researching payment and settlement alternatives, consulting with professional help, and learning legal rights will help people manage their medical debts and achieve financial stability.

Credit for Small Business Owners

To the small business owner, the credit world is both a challenge and an opportunity. Knowing the credit management issues is vital in managing personal credit and even using financial resources to expand and keep a business going. The peculiarity of the situation of small business owners is that their finances, both personal and business, are connected, and a good credit profile is essential.

Separating personal and business finances is one of the first steps undertaken by small business owners. This is the division that is employed to ensure personal credit rating against business liability and vice versa. To start a business credit profile, you need to get a federal tax identification number, open a business bank account, and get a business credit card. These measures not only assist in establishing a business credit history but also in managing cash flow in a better way.

Another important area of credit management that small business owners need to take care of is managing cash flow. Sound cash flow will help ensure that funds are available to make payments as they are due without delays, which will have a negative impact on credit ratings. There are ways to use a business credit card in order to keep a good credit score and, at the same time, enjoy rewards and benefits that credit card companies provide. Some of the ways to do so are by clearing the balance at the end of the month and also using credit cards to take advantage of the rewards and benefits provided by credit card companies.

It is also advisable that the owners of small businesses should understand how credit inquiries would affect their credit ratings. Whenever a business seeks a new line of credit, it goes under a hard inquiry, and this has the temporary effect of reducing credit scores. That is why it is best to have a limited number of credit applications and to have options that do not involve a hard inquiry where feasible.

Trade credit is also another tool that the owners of small businesses can use. Trade credit is used when businesses use the money to buy goods and services and pay them in the future. This is also a good idea to keep cash flow going, as the business will look good on credit reports with timely payments. Business owners need to develop good relations with their suppliers and agree on generous terms of credit.

Small business owners should also check credit reports on a regular basis. Monitoring personal and business credit reports will also assist in detecting any anomalies or fraud cases at an early stage. It can then be disputed and rectified within a reasonable time period. A good number of credit reporting agencies have monitoring services that can make owners of businesses aware of any differences in their credit reports.

Finally, when credit management is too hectic, an owner of a small business should take professional advice. Credit counselors and financial advisors might provide some tips according to the specific situation that a business is in and leave the decision-making to the business owners, who will make sound decisions without falling into the usual pitfalls.

In summary, the most important aspect of running a small business is sustaining a healthy credit profile because it can determine whether the small business owner will be able to raise capital, offer better terms, and ultimately expand the business. Small business owners can ensure that they have the financial flexibility they need to take opportunities and overcome difficulties by managing their credit effectively.

Young Adults and Credit Establishment

A good credit base in the complex world of personal finance is a very important thing to have as a young adult. Due to the newfound independence and financial responsibility that characterize this stage of life, opportunities and challenges arise when it comes to effective management of credit. When knowing the ins and outs of credit management, a safe financial future may become possible.

Young adults often find themselves between the school setting and the working world, where the issue of financial literacy takes center stage. A lot of people enter credit with student loans or even the temptation of their first credit card. Such early credit experiences can have a huge impact on your financial future. The trick is to look at these opportunities strategically, though, and realize that credit is not simply a matter of taking money but gaining trust with financial institutions.

The identification of the credit scores is one of the basic elements of credit establishment. These scores are a numerical representation of one's creditworthiness and affect things as simple as loan approvals and interest rates. With young adults, developing a good credit score at the beginning of their lives can be beneficial in getting favorable conditions on other financial services like mortgages or car loans. One has to understand the factors influencing credit scores, such as payment history, credit utilization, credit history length, type of credit in use, and credit inquiries.

The most considerable part of a credit score is payment history, which proves that it is important to pay bills on time. A missed payment may make a lasting impression even once, yet young adults must pay particular attention to this element of their financial behavior. Where feasible, automation of payment can assist in establishing a steady payment history, which in turn may strengthen the credit rating of an individual over time.

Another important factor is the use of credit, or the relationship between the credit drawn and the credit available. Having a low utilization rate, preferably less than 30, is an indicator to lenders that you are a responsible borrower. Young adults are expected to be keen on their expenditure habits to avoid spending their balance to the end of the available credit lines, which will reflect negatively on their ratings.

Credit history is also a factor in credit scoring. Though young adults have an edge based on their age only, early usage of a secured credit card or authorized usage of an account belonging to a family member can assist in building a credit history. Those measures may provide a stepping stone, so that young adults will graduate to more conventional credit products when they show responsible credit behavior.

Various forms of credit, including installment loans and revolving credit, have a positive impact on a credit profile. As their finances stabilize, young adults must think about diversification of their credit portfolio. Diversification of this nature can demonstrate economic stability and reliability to financial institutions.

Last but not least, caution with regard to new credit applications must also be taken into consideration. Every credit request would mean a hard inquiry that would temporarily drop the credit score. Young adults must be tactical in seeking new credit to ensure that the new credit matches their financial intentions and objectives.

These and some other values can help young adults be well-grounded in their future finances. Good credit does not come overnight; it takes time, hard work, and adherence to responsible financial behavior. Young adults are able to make good decisions and successfully navigate the intricacies of credit with the knowledge and proper equipment to ensure a successful financial future.

11

ADVANCED CREDIT STRATEGIES

Leveraging Credit for Investments

When it comes to personal finance, credit tends to be a key component among people trying to increase their level of investment. Learning to use credit can help open opportunities that otherwise may not be available. In its most basic form, leveraging credit entails borrowing capital and using it to maximize returns on investments. This plan has the potential to increase financial performance, but a high level of risk management and planning should support it.

Identifying the nature of credit and its suitability in different investment ventures is the initial move in tapping credit to invest. Some typical types of credit that people may want to consider include credit cards, personal loans, and home equity lines of credit (HELOCs). They have different terms, interests, and repayment expectations that should be properly considered against the backdrop of the target investment.

Although credit cards are easy to obtain, their interest rates tend to be very high and can offset investment returns very easily unless they are used carefully. However, when applied strategically in short-term investments that offer high returns, they may be an option. However, personal loans can be charged with a lower interest rate, and the repayment will be more scheduled and easier to handle in the long term. The benefit of HELOCs is that they enable one to take loans based on the value of their homes at relatively low-interest rates compared to an unsecured loan. This may be very useful in cases where there is a large source of investment that has high capital needs.

After choosing the right type of credit, the second most important thing is the investment. Not every investment would be appropriate to leverage credit. The investment should pay off more than the cost of borrowing. An example of leveraging credit is real estate, which could be a good investment because it is likely to appreciate and be rented. Equally, credit could be worth using when investing in a business or start-up when the business concept shows good growth and profitability.

Risk management is one of the factors that must be considered when investing in credit. The investor should be ready to face a situation when the investment fails to give the anticipated returns. It is possible to design a powerful risk management plan with definite financial goals, market dynamics, and contingency plans. This could be in the form of a cash buffer that can be employed to settle the loans in case of an investment slide or diversify the assets of the investment in order to dilute the risk to other factors and maintain a check over the investment plans and rectify the plans as per the market environment.

In addition, having a good credit score is very important when using credit to make investments. Having a good credit score will not only make it more likely to get a loan, but it will also get better loan terms. To make their credit profile appealing to lenders, investors must first make their repayments on time and maintain a low credit usage ratio.

The possible higher returns that come with taking a credit to invest are accompanied by higher risk. It requires a disciplined approach, adequate market research, and absolute commitment to financial accountability. Given the complexity of credit products and matching them with well-studied investment opportunities, individuals can easily capitalize on the power of credit to improve their financial portfolios.

Optimizing Credit for Major Purchases

The strategic management of credit is of primary importance when considering a major purchase. It is not just about access to finances, but knowing the finer details of using credit and its financial aspects in general. The initial move in this procedure is an exhaustive analysis of their credit status. This would involve getting and analyzing credit reports to determine accuracy and areas that can be improved. Any inconsistencies must then be resolved quickly, since they may negatively impact credit scores, which are the determining factor in obtaining good loan conditions.

The other crucial factor is the time required for credit activities. It is also prudent not to use new credit accounts or charge up on an existing line of credit before making a big purchase. The reason is that these activities have the short-term effect of reducing credit scores by boosting credit utilization ratios and adding hard inquiries to credit reports. Rather, the emphasis is to pay off the current debt. The reduction of outstanding balances not only increases the utilization rate of credit but also improves the overall creditworthiness.

In addition, it is important to know the various kinds of credit scores and how they affect them. FICO scores are very popular, but Vantage Score is also taken into consideration by many lenders. Knowledge of the scoring models of prospective lenders can help an individual narrow down their efforts to the most important areas of their credit profiles. Also, there is a positive impact of having a balanced mix of credit accounts, like revolving credit and installment loans, on the credit scores. This must, however, be balanced with the requirement of ensuring that credit inquiries are kept to a minimum.

There are also options available to those who have poor credit to improve their position ahead of a big purchase. A secured credit card or credit-builder loan can help rebuild credit. What makes these products creditworthy is that when responsibly used, they may cause credit scores to increase with time. Another good idea is to become an authorized user on the credit card account of a responsible person, as this can also help in developing a good credit history.

The other important factor is the negotiation of the terms of the loan. With a good knowledge of his credit profile, one is better placed to negotiate a good loan. This involves interest rates, required loan amount, and repayment terms. You should always compare offers with other lenders so as to get the best deal possible. It is crucial to know the terms and conditions of any credit agreement to prevent any unforeseen expenses or penalties that may affect financial well-being.

Last but not least, planning and budgeting are also vital. To make sure that paying monthly is affordable, it is always good to create a detailed budget that includes the new purchase and all the costs related to it. This proactive measure can help not only to make sure payments are made on time, which is crucial to maintaining a good credit score, but also to make sure that funds are not stretched to the limit of skipping payment and potentially causing credit damage.

To sum up, optimizing credit on major purchases is a complex task that requires proper planning, credit management, and decision-making. Being aware of these principles and implementing them will allow them to achieve better credit scores, secure better loan terms, and achieve their financial goals more effectively.

Using Credit Wisely in Retirement

There is a delicate balance between being economically secure and having financial freedom in the landscape of credit during retirement, and a willingness to navigate it requires a keen, strategic approach. When a person gets into this life stage, the role played by credit changes and requires the person to change the manner in which they handle and use credit. Staying financially viable and adapting to potentially fixed or limited income streams turns out to be the big purpose.

The first thing to do is to reevaluate the need to use credit in day-to-day financial undertakings. The use of credit during retirement should, in an ideal state, be reduced since earnings earned at work are reduced. This step promotes the use of savings and other fixed-income resources such as pensions or social security. However, it is also important to have a good credit score, which can impact the cost of borrowing, insurance, and even accommodation.

The retirees should know what they need in credit and the resources they have before they can use their credit wisely. This will include a comprehensive examination of all credit accounts, so that they conform to the current financial interests and requirements. We need to review the conditions of the credit card or loan, taking into account things such as interest rates, fees, and rewards. Retirees must focus on the accounts that will benefit them the most at the least possible cost and close the ones that are unnecessary or expensive.

The other consideration of prudent credit management in retirement is ensuring that one has a low credit utilization ratio. This is by maintaining the balances in credit cards as low as possible compared with the credit limits, preferably below 30%. Not only does this help maintain a healthy credit score, but it also helps cut down on the interest bill, which is especially helpful when the income is fixed.

It is important to keep track of credit. It is a good practice for retirees to review their credit reports at least once a year to detect any errors or unauthorized transactions that may negatively affect their credit ratings. By using free credit monitoring services, they will be able to detect any major fluctuation or suspicious activity and take necessary actions in time.

Moreover, it is reasonable to borrow to spend on one big and calculated expenditure rather than buying daily commodities. This project helps in the management of the cash flow by avoiding interest payments and also has a backup in case of emergencies. An example of this is a major home repair or medical bill, planned and budgeted, which is easier to meet using credit rather than savings.

Consolidation is also good among the retirees who have several high-interest credit cards. Debt consolidation may make finances easier and may even reduce the interest rates, making it easier to pay monthly. However, consolidation should be done cautiously and should be confined to the long-term financial plans and not extended indefinitely till its objective is fulfilled.

Finally, the development of a relationship with a financial advisor may be priceless. These experts are able to provide personalized guidance on how to use credit, maximize retirement benefits, and spend later on in life. One of the methods to ensure that the control of credit applies to the new financial environment and individual aims is regular consultation.

In a nutshell, wisely spending credit in retirement is a fine balancing act between preserving a good credit score and keeping money safe. This time and its features will allow the retirees to live through and manage with self-confidence and financial security due to the needs, management of credit usage, and professional consultation.

Credit as a Wealth-Building Tool

The use of credit is an effective tool towards achieving financial expansion and stability, providing people with a chance to improve their wealth in the long term. This is because, through knowing and strategically using credit, doors can be opened to opportunities that were not necessarily available. Credit is not merely a lending and borrowing money technique, but a means that could lead to a great monetary improvement when applied in the right manner.

The keys to credit as a tool of wealth creation are based on how it works and what it can do. Credit also allows a person to access funds, which can be invested in appreciating assets, like real estate or education, and that can bring returns much more than the cost of borrowing. It is no ordinary use of credit, but a long-run choice that is informed by the knowledge of the interest rate, terms of repayment, and long-term cost of borrowing.

The main advantage of credit is that it gives leverage. Leverage enables people to manage more with very little of their own capital. A mortgage would be a good example in the real estate sector when a borrower is able to buy a piece of property that is well beyond the value of the down payment. The more the property goes up in value, the more equity the owner has, and this could bring in a lot of money in the long run. This recognition can be a pillar of wealth creation as it can be of both short-term and long-term value.

In addition, having a good credit profile will result in increased borrowing conditions, including reduced interest rates and increased credit limits. Such positive conditions make borrowing cheaper and the ability to invest in additional wealth-generating activities higher. A good credit report is generally regarded as an indicator of financial responsibility. Therefore, it becomes easier to get loans to invest or start business activities that produce more sources of income.

Further, credit may play a critical role in cash flow and liquidity management. Connection to sources of credit is also significant to the entrepreneur because he or she may get access to the money they need to utilize the opportunities within the business or address the swings of the market without necessarily emptying his or her pockets. Such flexibility could be paramount in sustaining and expanding a business, which ultimately leads to wealth creation in the long term.

However, there should also be discipline and strategy in the right use of credit. We need to distinguish between good and bad debt; the former is employed to purchase items that increase in value or earn us a living, whereas the latter is employed to purchase items that we consume without adding any monetary value to them. This knowledge can be used to make rational decisions that can contribute to achieving financial objectives.

Maximizing the wealth-building potential of credit should mean that individuals using credit products need to embrace practices like checking their credit reports on a regular basis, maintaining low credit utilization ratios, and ensuring they make payments on time. Not only do they increase credit scores, but they also demonstrate financial dependability to lenders, which increases borrowing opportunities even more.

Overall, credit can be an effective accelerator of wealth creation when it is utilized wisely. It allows one to access the opportunity to acquire assets, expand the business, and become financially stable. People can achieve financial freedom and success by using credit prudently and using it in a way that demonstrates good credit characteristics. The balancing act, in this case, is strategic credit and financial responsibility and long-term planning.

12

THE EMOTIONAL SIDE OF CREDIT MANAGEMENT

Overcoming Credit-Related Anxiety

Credit life is a frightening experience that sometimes seems like an uphill task to navigate, and anxiety covers every turn. The very idea of working with credit reports, scores, and debt can make many people feel a surge of stress and confusion. The feeling is not new, and the anxiety surrounding credit is the fear of the unknown and its possible aftermath.

The first thing that will help you to overcome this anxiety is to know that you are not the only person who feels this way. Apprehensions are common in many people, and the ability to recognize this can be comforting. The fear of credit is usually the result of a lack of knowledge or awareness regarding how credit systems work and how credit scores influence the financial life of individuals. With the right education, this fear will be empowered.

The first step is to learn the fundamentals of credit. The mystery can be unpuzzled by understanding the elements that make up your credit score, including payment history, credit utilization, length of credit history, types of credit used, and recent credit enquiries. This will help you realize that credit scores are not a random assessment of what you are worth based on how you manage money, but are a mirror image of particular financial habits.

The other key thing to consider in conquering your credit-related anxiety is being proactive in managing your credit health. Start by obtaining your credit report from the three big credit bureaus: Experian, Equifax, and TransUnion. Looking over these reports once a year will keep you up-to-date on your credit and identify any errors that could require corrections. Gaining access to what is in your credit report can help ease the fear of reality hitting you, and it will also help you feel in control.

It is also important that you formulate a plan to deal with any negative items on your credit report. There are situations when the person holds the creditors at bay, when the person is negotiating the payment, or when the person is trying to settle the debt. In each of these cases, a strategy will help him/her to feel less powerless than feeling helpless, which comes with credit anxiety. Also, positive financial habits, which include paying bills on time, maintaining low credit card balances, and avoiding unnecessary credit checks, can slowly fix your credit score and increase confidence.

In addition, there is a need to cultivate a proper attitude towards credit management. This includes redefining the perspective of a setback. Rather than viewing them as failures, view them as learning opportunities that offer useful lessons about making financial decisions in the future. To keep you motivated as you work towards achieving better credit health, building strength, and having a positive mindset can be helpful.

Support systems are also important in dealing with credit-related anxiety. It can be money management classes, internet discussion rooms, or support networks, but having someone to talk to about your situation and share tips on managing it can be very helpful. By telling people about your experience and sharing ideas, you can increase your determination to make it through credit issues.

Finally, remember that repairing your credit is a time-consuming task. The main thing is perseverance and patience. Mark milestones on the path along the way, as this helps to achieve success in the long run. These measures will help you eliminate the fear of credit problems and transform them into a controllable part of your fiscal condition, which will result in increased economic stability and serenity.

Building Confidence in Financial Decisions

Weaving through the terrain of financial choices has become a journey of mysteries and indecision. Developing confidence in financial choices is a blend of personal learning, identifying objectives, and creating an atmosphere that is conducive to positive decisions. The initial step in this process is to know the basic provisions behind credit and financial management. Power is knowledge, and once the veil is lifted over the financial concept, one can make their financial choices with confidence and understanding.

An essential element of establishing such confidence is to establish a realistic and attainable financial objective. Setting short-term goals to meet the long-term goals will be the way to financial success. This is done by developing a budget that is not only responsive to the present but also responsive to future costs as well as cost-saving opportunities. Breaking down big financial objectives into small steps will allow individuals to monitor their progress and make informed corrections when needed.

In addition, the contribution of technology to the empowerment of financial decision-making cannot be overemphasized. Keeping a realistic perspective of personal finances can be achieved using budgeting software programs and credit rating programs. These applications provide alerts and notifications that remind and keep users aware and involved in their financial transactions, minimizing the chances of missed payments or excessive spending.

Along with technological support, it is important to create a favorable network. An individual can also consider visiting financial advisors, joining community groups, or accessing online forums to get quality information and inspiration. These networks bring together this sense of community and learning, and individuals can share tips, experiences, and support one another in their financial journey.

The emotional aspect of making financial decisions is an area that is usually ignored. Confidence is not only a question of knowledge but also of mentality. Having a positive mindset towards financial management and learning to take failure as a learning experience and celebrating small wins can go a long way to boosting confidence. This change of attitude fosters a spirit of looking beyond to resolve financial setbacks.

Second, one should be aware of the psychological barriers to making confident financial choices. Awareness of fear or anxiety patterns that occur with money helps people confront these problems directly. This could mean consulting an expert, taking financial classes, or just taking time to analyze how one has made financial choices and the consequences of those choices.

Finally, confidence can also be strengthened through the ability to see success and have a clear perspective of long-term goals. Developing visual representations like progress charts or vision boards might be an effective constant reminder of financial targets and accomplishments. Not only do they encourage, but they also provide physical expression to the process of financial empowerment.

To conclude, the development of confidence in financial decisions is a complex process that includes the acquisition of knowledge, the formulation of goals, the use of technologies, community support, and a positive attitude. When combined, people will be able to navigate their financial environment with greater confidence and generate the financial results they want.

Resilience in the Face of Setbacks

Sailing through the stormy seas of credit management can often lead to setbacks and a difficult ordeal. They are not obstacles, but landmarks which can be called an ordeal of strength and elasticity. In the event of a failure, either through circumstances beyond one's control or personal mistakes, it is important to rethink the failures as lessons and developmental opportunities. The credit recovery phenomenon is non-linear in nature and will have peaks and troughs, but every decline is a stepping stone to a stronger financial future.

Another important component of bouncing back is the ability to reframe disappointments as learning opportunities. This change of perspective turns the story of defeat into one of empowerment. It is possible to explore causes of a setback and draw insights and lessons that inform future choices. This not only helps in the short-term recovery but also helps to strengthen the financial habits in the long-term.

Take examples of people who have bounced back after losses in their finances. These are not only stories of credit score restoration, but also accounts of confidence and self-efficacy restoration. Incidentally, credit conquerors are known to say that a combination of planning, introspection, and the resetting of realistic goals has aided their credit revivals. These tales are useful reminders that failures are not final moments, but instead, they are turning points in the credit management process.

Some practical activities like journaling and self-reflection may be important to restore confidence following a financial slip. A setback can be clarified and directed by writing down three major lessons learned. Also, it is important to set new short-term goals to stay on track and motivated. These objectives must be achievable and quantifiable to give one a sense of direction and an accomplishment when each milestone is attained.

Another useful instrument that could help to manage the situation in the face of financial problems is the creation of a setback recovery plan. This plan must consider the analysis of the setback, how to overcome the setback, and a timeline for overcoming the setback. This kind of plan is not only structural but is also motivational and reminds people of their potential to surmount all obstacles.

In addition, the tools, checklists, and support networks should be revisited and used again. These resources are invaluable during times of failure, as they give some form of direction and inspiration. Be it through the reuse of dispute logs, templates, or consulting accountability partners, these tools are meant to help individuals get on their feet again.

Finally, the messages and calls to action promote performance and encourage trust, which will be more successful in the long run. Even simple sentences like, my credit is a work in progress and so am I remind me that there must be growth and development at all times. Each of the small moves will contribute to the bigger goal of financial empowerment and financial resilience.

Credit management is a challenging task, but the ability to stick through it amidst the adversities is the key to success. Taking failures as an opportunity to become a better person, treating injuries effectively, and thinking positively about financial problems can help people overcome their difficulties and feel safe and stronger than before.

Empowering Others with Your Journey

The story of credit troubles disposition and the subsequent attainment of a safe economic footing is an extremely intimate account that is eminently familiar to various individuals. This transformation not only leads to personal achievement but also gives one a priceless chance to serve as an example and mentor to others who might be going through the same journey. Telling personal stories of successes and failures in credit repair can bring us together in a supportive community and give others the strength to take the steps to achieve financial independence.

Sharing personal stories of how one overcomes credit challenges is one of the most successful methods of empowering others. These may be powerful narratives about struggles and survivability. People can provide guidance and support to those who may feel alone in their fight by sharing with them the obstacles they have encountered and how they have managed these challenges. There are personal accounts that can simplify the credit repair process and make it less daunting for other individuals.

It is important to help people take charge of their credit by creating an environment of mutual support. Creating community organizations or becoming members of established organizations can be a good place to share experiences and resources. Those groups are virtual, like social media groups and online forums, or physical, including local meet-ups. In these kinds of societies, people can give each other tips, talk about their blessings, and offer emotional encouragement to others, and this creates a sense of community strength that motivates people to continue despite the storms they are going through.

Another way in which accountability partnerships can be empowering is through the empowerment of others. They can assign each other some goals to achieve, monitor their progress, and hold each other accountable by having a credit buddy. Such cooperation can be especially helpful in ensuring motivation and focus, due to the formation of a sense of overall responsibility and devotion to the credit betterment process.

Visual aids like progress charts and milestones can truly play a significant role in empowering a person. Clear, achievable objectives are set, and objective means of measuring progress are provided using examples of these tools. Through small successes on the journey, morale can be lifted and positive actions reinforced. This can be seen through getting rewarded on a personal level after reaching a better credit score or disputing an error in a bill, which will only serve as an additional incentive to work harder and perform better.

Another way to empower is to encourage others to learn to manage their credit. By providing access to resources like books, workshops, and online courses, they can impart knowledge and tools that can help people take control of their credit. Education helps people to become confident and self-sufficient so that they can make wise choices and prevent common mistakes.

Finally, the credit betterment process is not only about personal achievements, but also about helping others. Through wisdom, encouragement, and a welcoming community, people are able to influence others to change their financial lives. Such community empowerment can help make a larger social change in society, in that there will be an increased number of individuals who will be able and willing to become self-reliant in regard to finances.

13

FUTURE TRENDS IN CREDIT AND FI-NANCE

The Impact of Technology on Credit

One of the determinants in the modern financial landscape that has altered the way individuals use and associate with credit is technology. Digital innovation, coupled with financial services, has not only changed the face of traditional banking but has also brought about new processes of credit management and accessibility. It has been characterized by the launch of online financial products, applications, and digital banking platforms that allow consumers to track their credit in real-time to offer the most convenient experience and control ever.

The democratization of financial information is one of the largest technological effects on credit. Now that it is easy to access your credit score and report through the services of online credit monitoring, people are able to manage their credit score and report with greater awareness of their personal finances. These websites give their customers extensive information about their credit situations, including issues that affect credit scores like payment record, credit usage, and age of credit activities. This openness not only leads to increased financial literacy but also pre-supposes active management of credit.

In addition, technology has transformed the process of applying for credit products. Long paperwork and visits to the banks are long behind us. These days, a consumer can apply for credit cards, loans, and other financial products online. In many situations, they get decisions online immediately, using advanced algorithms that determine a consumer's creditworthiness within minutes. This not only simplifies things for the consumers but also simplifies the operations of financial institutions to the advantage of both parties.

Mobile technology has also brought in a sense of flexibility and accessibility never before imagined. Banking applications and mobile wallets enable users to monitor their finances in real time, including such features as notifications about transactions, splitting purchases into categories, and budgeting. The tools assist individuals in keeping up with their financial obligations and minimizing the chances of defaulting on their payments, which negatively impacts their credit ratings.

In addition, the introduction of artificial intelligence and machine learning into the financial service industry has promoted the personalization of credit products even further. These technologies work with large amounts of data to personalize financial products to individual needs, forecasting credit behaviour, and providing individualized financial guidance. These will, in addition, not only make customers have a higher level of satisfaction, but also, in the process, more responsible lending practices will be born as the lenders will be more able to predict risk, and be able to give credit to those who will most likely manage it positively.

The technological revolution in credit management is not without its problems, however. Financial services are going digital, which raises the question of data security and privacy. The more personal information is stored and processed over the Internet, the higher the chance of cyberattacks and data breaches, which requires effective security protocols to safeguard sensitive consumer information.

In conclusion, it is safe to say that technology has transformed the credit environment in certain ways, providing the consumer with increased control and knowledge of their financial health. Although the benefits of these developments are obvious, they also require an increase in security concern awareness and resolve to protect personal information. With the continually changing world of technology, there will definitely be more innovations in credit management that will empower customers in their financial endeavors.

Evolving Credit Scoring Models

Over the years, the credit scoring landscape has seen major changes in response to changing financial habits and technological changes that define modern society. When credit scoring first began, it was a very primitive process with a lot of reliance on the human eye and limited data, which often led to a subjective assessment process. With the automated credit scoring models coming in, all financial institutions started demanding more efficient and proper means of credit scoring.

FICO credit scoring systems were ahead of the pack and offered a generalized method of grading credit. These models mainly relied on statistical analysis, using information points like payment history, credit utilization, length of credit history, types of credit accounts, and recent inquiries. The FICO-created industry standard was straightforward to implement and apply since it included an objective risk that was measurable, resulting in more objective lending decisions.

With the advancements in the digital age, credit scoring models have become more advanced. This was altered as Vantage Score came out in the mid-2000s as an alternative to FICO with a variant algorithm and a score range. Vantage Score was special because it relied on a wider range of data sets, and it was updated more often, thus providing a more dynamic view of the behaviour of one particular person as it relates to credit.

Alternative data has been one of the most important developments in credit scoring. The majority of traditional models have been pegged to financial transactions. Still, the new trends have expanded the data set to incorporate some non-traditional data such as utility payments, rental history, and even social media activity. Such an evolution should provide a more comprehensive view of the financial activity of a consumer, particularly those with poor credit histories, also known as credit invisibles.

Credit scoring has been revolutionized even further with the development of artificial intelligence and machine learning. The technologies make it possible to analyze more complex sets of data and help to construct predictive models that can predict credit risk better. Machine learning algorithms can constantly update their evaluations with new information to become more precise as time goes by. This flexibility is important in a time when consumerism and economic situations have the potential to change quickly.

Moreover, transparency and the availability of information to the consumer have improved in another area, credit scoring democracy. Most credit scoring agencies have made credit scores and report available free of charge, and it has given individuals the power to be in control of their financial health. The result of this transparency is an enlightened consumer population, resulting in an effective use of credit and the reduction of the possibility of making a financial mistake.

This notwithstanding, there are still challenges. The privacy and accuracy of data concerns are continuous problem that must be addressed. To preserve consumer trust, it is crucial that credit scoring models are void of any biases and that they are, in fact, regulated.

Finally, credit scoring models also capture the fact that there is a general inclusivity and precision trend in financial services. As technology continues to climb, credit scoring has the potential to become increasingly personalized and offer personalized financial solutions that can address the needs of individual consumers. Not only does this put lenders in a better position to reduce risk, but it also arms consumers with the knowledge and ability to man oeuvre their financial lives constructively.

Regulatory Changes Ahead

A series of regulatory changes is impending to make navigating the landscape of credit management all the more dynamic. These developments will transform the reporting and management of credit and affect consumers and financial institutions. To understand whether it is possible to control its credit profile and how these changes can impact personal treatment of finance, these changes should be understood.

Among the major changes is in how credit bureaus resolve disputes. Previously, consumers have had a difficult time fighting inaccuracies in their credit reports and have had to deal with long processes and flawed results. It is anticipated that the new regulations will simplify such processes and require credit bureaus to respond much faster and at a higher rate. This will enhance the consumers, as this will imply that all the wrong information in the credit report will be corrected immediately, and the accuracy of the credit report will thus increase.

Besides the advancements in dispute management, changes are imminent in the area of access and use of credit information. The reforms will promote privacy and data security among consumers. As more people worry about breaches of data and identity theft, the new laws will create greater limitations on who has access to credit information and in which situations. This will likely secure sensitive information better and provide more peace of mind to the consumer.

Additionally, there will be improvements in the ways credit scores are calculated in the regulatory environment. Its purpose is to allow a more extensive and impartial evaluation of the creditworthiness of a consumer. These will be changes that incorporate a wider spectrum of financial patterns and data, beyond the old metrics of payment history and outstanding debt. New scoring models are developed to reveal a more comprehensive portrait of the financial habits of a person by uniting such factors as rent and utility payments.

Legislators are also looking into the practices of collection agencies. New regulations will restrict the aggressive collection practices and demand increased transparency of communications. Consumers will be empowered to have transparent and easy access to clear and detailed information about their debts, how they were calculated, and their charges. It is hoped that such openness will help minimize confusion and conflicts between the consumer and the collector and encourage a more respectful and knowledgeable conversation.

Financial literacy and education are also a priority. The reforms below will encourage financial institutions to offer educational resources and tools to empower consumers to learn and manage their credit better. It is a prevention intervention that is anchored on empowering individuals regarding good financial decisions that will eventually translate to better credit management and financial status.

These rules can be seen as part of a wider trend in consumer empowerment and consumer protection in the credit marketplace. Knowing this and becoming accustomed to these new rules, perhaps people can more efficiently plan their financial future because they will know their credit rating at all times. We are now moving into a period where consumers will need to use these new resources and protections, turning to them to increase their financial resilience and security.

Preparing for a Cashless Society

Not only is the shift towards a cashless society close at hand, but it is also a reality that needs to be prepared for and dealt with. With the rising use of digital transactions, citizens need to be aware of the consequences of this change and how to live in the changing world of finances.

The decrease in cash use can be traced back to the daily transactions, as digital payment is becoming the standard. This is brought about by the development of technology, which has made electronic transactions more secure, convenient, and efficient. As phones get smarter, payments become less physical, and more and more banks are going online, the ability of the consumer to control their money without touching the physical cash is increasing.

Digital payment systems are becoming important as people strive to transact without the use of cash. The only way to be included in this new economy will be to be familiar with mobile payment applications, online banking platforms, and digital wallets. They enable the customers to do their transactions within a shorter period, monitor their expenditures in real-time, and even automate some of their financial tasks, making them more financially savvy and in control of their expenses.

A cashless society is a place where security is a major issue. Cyber threats are on the rise as more and more financial transactions are going digital. People need to be careful about securing their financial data with strong, unique passwords and with multi-factor authentication where it exists. Frequently reviewing account statements and credit reports will allow for identifying unauthorized transactions in the initial stages of harm reduction.

Another challenge pertaining to data privacy is the shift to a cashless society. Online transactions produce huge volumes of information, and it is important to handle this information responsibly. Financial institutions and third-party service providers should inform consumers about the ways in which their data is gathered, stored, and used. Knowledge about privacy rights and rights to access and correct data can help people control their personal data.

Another significant part of the transition to a cashless society is financial inclusion. On the one hand, digital payment is convenient. Still, on the other hand, it has the disadvantage of marginalizing people who do not have access to the required technology or banking facilities. They should work towards making digital financial services available to every sector of society. This means making the internet accessible to more people, making internet devices affordable, and providing financial literacy classes to teach the population how to conduct digital transactions.

To the business, going digital with no cash means more than only accepting electronic payments. It involves implementing digital payment systems in their operations, having strong cybersecurity, and keeping up with the changing payment technologies. Companies that adopt such changes have the potential to improve the customer experience and streamline their operations, and possibly cut down costs incurred in moving cash.

Governments and other regulatory authorities also have an important role to play in ensuring a seamless change to a cashless society. Regulations that assure consumers that their transactions over the internet are safe, their personal information is private, and financial services are accessible are required. The approach to cooperation between government and business can become the engine of innovation without an unsafe and uneven financial environment.

To sum it up, to be ready to live in a cashless society, one has to know and accept technology in the financial industry. It requires an aggressive approach to security, awareness of issues relating to data privacy, and a willingness to become financially inclusive. Having the tools and knowledge needed to navigate a cashless world, people and companies can succeed in the digital revolution and not become victims of a cashless economy.

14

CONCLUSION AND NEXT STEPS

Summarizing Key Takeaways

The journey to mastering credit is a collection of conscious actions and thought-provoking discoveries, all aimed at empowering individuals in their financial stories. The process starts by learning the complex system of credit systems, and the functions of major players in the credit systems, like credit lenders, credit bureaus, and data furnishers. The ability to identify the interaction of these components offers a baseline of information that allows a person to negotiate the credit environment with more confidence and clarity.

The most important thing about credit management is the knowledge of the factors that contribute to credit scores. People can determine areas of improvement by dissecting their factors, such as payment history, credit utilization, history of credit, credit mix, and inquiries on new credit. This kind of knowledge will enable taking significant action that will have a long-term impact, making a positive difference to credit scores, which is worth the necessity to be regular and make decisions on the basis of relevant information.

Myths and misconceptions tarnish the story of credit repair and can sabotage the best intentions. Busting these myths, like the idea that having a balance in your wallet is better than getting credit or that all debt is gone after seven years, is a way that can help people concentrate on practical action plans that can produce actual outcomes. The process can be further demystified by understanding the distinction between soft and hard inquiries, as well as understanding that income is not a component of credit scores.

One of the most important elements of a good credit score is to be aware of fraud and unscrupulous behavior. Education about the pitfalls to avoid, including scams to repair your credit and other types of miraculous solutions, will give people the tools to defend themselves and make wiser decisions. With this type of knowledge, people will be able to recognize red flags and avoid any deals that sound too good to be true.

Credit management empowerment also depends on being able to challenge mistakes on credit reports effectively. It is important to know how to access the free credit reports of all three major bureaus and to be familiar with the structure and contents of the credit report. The information can guide the individual to identify errors and rectify them, thus showing their credit history.

The only way to develop a strong credit future is by developing means and systems that supplement financial well-being in the long run. Strategies that can help to rebuild credit include using secured credit cards and being added as an authorized user on a trusted account. Keeping credit low and paying punctually are both habits that can help in creating a strong credit image.

Lastly, credit management is not a process that one should go through alone. Creating a support network of accountability companions, friends, families, and internet communities provides support and wisdom. Marking milestones and recognizing progress enables the creation of a positive mindset that supports the belief that each action taken will be a step towards financial empowerment and freedom.

Patience, knowledge, and perseverance are the keys to credit mastery. Knowing the game, busting myths, avoiding fraud, and using tools and support systems may help people to take ownership of their credit and ultimately their finances.

Your Personal Action Plan

Developing a personal credit enhancement action plan is a goal-oriented and considered process, depending on specific situations. It starts with an in-depth evaluation of your present state of credit, which is the starting point of creating a realistic and successful plan. This includes getting your credit report (or reports from all three major bureaus) and paying attention to any mistakes and outdated information, along with any red flags like high utilization or delinquency reports.

After you clearly understand your credit status, you then need to establish certain goals that are specific but achievable. These can be reducing balances on your credit card, establishing automatic payments to make sure that bills are paid on time, or challenging mistakes in your credit report. Any goal must be quantifiable so that you can measure improvement along the way and modify your approach accordingly.

In order to sustain your own action plan, you need to create a budget. All income and expenditures must be included in this budget, and the areas to reduce must be made conspicuous so that you can spare some money to pay off the debt or save. Things such as budgeting applications or spreadsheets can also come in really handy to help you monitor your spending and keep you on course to achieve your financial targets.

The act of visualizing a timeline for each goal brings structure and encouragement to your course of action. Having timelines to settle certain debts or attain specific milestones in your credit score can help you stay focused and give you a sense of achievement as you accomplish each mark. You need to be able to bend with the times and change up your schedule as situations evolve, but you need to maintain an upward momentum.

The efficacy of your plan can be improved by adding elements of accountability. This can be as simple as telling a close friend or family member about your goals, and allowing him/her to help you out by giving you tips and support, or being part of an online community where you can share your tips and experiences with other individuals going through the same process.

One of the most important parts of your action plan is to monitor your credit score and reports on a regular basis. This helps you to monitor your progress, detect any emerging problems, and be able to act on them instantaneously. To help keep up with changes in your credit report, lots of services include free or low-cost credit monitoring services, which can give you alerts so you stay on track.

Besides this, educating yourself in matters related to credit makes you more informed in making decisions. The way you use your credit, like paying and spending, influences your credit score, so when you know what affects your credit score, you can focus on actions that will make the largest positive difference. Books, webinars, financial counseling, etc., can enhance your level of knowledge and help you better manage credit issues.

Lastly, it is important to celebrate small achievements along the way to stay motivated. Positive reinforcement is recognizing and rewarding yourself when you accomplish a goal, whether it is paying off a credit card or increasing your credit score.

With a specific and individualized action plan, you will be able to control your credit future, turning obstacles into opportunities to grow and become financially empowered. Not only does this proactive method help you increase your credit score, but it also helps you improve your financial health more generally, which opens the door to greater financial freedom and stability.

Staying Motivated for the Long Haul

When dealing with credit management and control over the long term, long-term motivation is a key success factor. Such an undertaking requires not just knowledge of financial concepts but also a strong determination to self-develop and to persevere. Credit improvement is often burdened with various challenges, which are challenging and, at the same time, test perseverance. Still, it is in the challenges that one finds a chance to get profound personal development.

A strong support system is one of the main tools used to maintain motivation. Friends, family, or even being part of online communities can help bring the support and motivation needed to keep themselves on track. These networks provide us with a pool of group knowledge and group power that makes us feel nourished when we stumble and celebrate with a crowd of other people. This can help a person feel a part of a community and less isolated on their financial path, which is also a big motivator.

Another useful way to keep momentum is to visualize the progress using tangible markers. Setting goals in an abstract form and visualizing them in charts or an app can help turn abstract goals into tangible ones. These visual reminders are meant not only to remind one of the progresses that he or she has made but also to keep moving forward. It is important to celebrate the smallest wins here, as they serve the purpose of positive reinforcement and can help to keep the momentum going and gain confidence.

Besides, having real and achievable goals is the key to remaining motivated. One of the ways to avoid feelings of overwhelm and make the process less intimidating is to break down the bigger goals into smaller, manageable ones. Even the simplest task, once completed, adds up to the bigger picture, providing a firm reinforcement that progress is underway. This gradual strategy will aid in ensuring that the motivation is not lost over time.

Besides these planning strategies, there should be an inculcation of a resilience and flexibility mindset. Putting a negative experience into perspective as a learning experience instead of a failure can turn what might otherwise have been a discouraging experience into a learning experience. This will foster growth thinking where misfortunes are seen as stepping stones to more knowledge and capacity. Such an attitude helps to remain motivated even in the most difficult situations, as every obstacle is a chance to rehearse and perform better, to become stronger.

The review and readjustment of strategies are other important features of maintaining motivation. The strategies change as the condition's changes and as the objectives change. Being rather flexible, the planning also makes it possible to provide a certain change based on the existing conditions and reality to make the work topical and significant. A regular re-examination of what is functioning and what is not will prevent stagnation and keep the journey interesting and alive.

In the end, maintaining long-term motivation in credit management is a question of cultivating a balance between discipline and flexibility, community support and individual accountability, short-term success and long vision. It involves a desire to learn continuously and change. With the combination of these factors in one mix, the journey to credit promotion becomes not only a financial task but a life-altering process of self-development and empowerment.

Final Words of Encouragement

Now that you are at the doorstep of a new financial life, you must accept the power and stamina that you have developed during this process. Look back, and think of what you have gone through, and what they all say to you is that you are a person who has been through fire and has come through. It is not a number on the page but a transformational journey of reclaiming your agency and building a future that aligns with your dreams and ambitions.

Empowerment of finances is a process that is learned over time. Your acquired knowledge is a starting point from which you can build a strong credit profile, one that portrays not only your financial well-being but also your dedication to constant enhancement. Keep in mind that the long road to credit recovery is not a sprint, but rather a marathon that will require time, discipline, and readiness to learn each point and turn.

Look at failures as learning opportunities and not as setbacks. Any weakness is a chance to train and master your technique, and any difficulties you may meet on your way are stepping stones to your success. You set yourself up to succeed in the future by cultivating a mentality that sees hardships as chances to learn, with the strength to come back even more resilient than before.

Be surrounded by a support circle. Whether it is family, friends, or even a community of like-minded people, having a support system can act as the motivating factor and remind us of the accountability we require to keep track. Your own stories and experiences can be shared with others and cause a ripple of change, empowerment, and learning that can positively impact everyone.

Be careful and watchful of your credit. Check your credit reports regularly, keep yourself updated on credit legislation, and watch out for those who defraud. You can ensure you do not lose what you have already achieved and ensure the future, as far as finance is concerned, is not jeopardized because of uncertainties by remaining informed and active.

Some of the best things to do are to celebrate your successes, even though they may be small. Every accomplishment, whether it is getting a better credit rating or paying off a loan, deserves celebration. You need to use these moments as a confirmation that you can and are making progress, which helps you keep going to achieve even higher levels.

Along the way, keep in mind that your financial fate is in your own hands. Your future is in your hands to create a world of your values and dreams using the tools and strategies that you have learned. Keep the momentum going and use your experience as a hope and a possibility.

I hope that in this continuing effort, you have the strength to dream big and the intelligence to make your way in the labyrinths of credit management with certainty and grace. Your credit is not a figure; it is your story, your struggle, and your consistent effort to achieve a life that is full and free of financial problems and issues. Take this new start positively and with resolve, but understand that you can shape your own financial future.